Better Homes and Gardens®

Low-Fat Bold Flavors

Better Homes and Gardens® Books
Des Moines, Iowa

Better Homes and Gardens® Books *An imprint of Meredith® Books*

Low-Fat Bold Flavors

Project Editor: Lisa Holderness

Contributing Editor: Spectrum Communication Services, Inc.

Contributing Designer: Conyers Design Collaborative, Inc.

Copy Chief: Catherine Hamrick

Copy and Production Editor: Terri Fredrickson

Contributing Proofreaders: Susan J. Kling, Sheila Mauck

Electronic Production Coordinator: Paula Forest

Editorial and Design Assistants: Judy Bailey, Karen Schirm

Test Kitchen Director: Lynn Blanchard

Production Director: Douglas M. Johnston

Production Manager: Pam Kvitne

Assistant Prepress Manager: Marjorie J. Schenkelberg

Meredith® Books

Editor in Chief: James D. Blume

Design Director: Matt Strelecki

Managing Editor: Gregory H. Kayko

Director, Sales & Marketing, Retail: Michael A. Peterson

Director, Sales & Marketing, Special Markets: Rita McMullen

Director, Sales & Marketing, Home & Garden Center Channel: Ray Wolf

Director, Operations: George A. Susral

Vice President, General Manager: Jamie L. Martin

Better Homes and Gardens® **Magazine**

Editor in Chief: Jean LemMon

Executive Food Editor: Nancy Byal

Meredith Publishing Group

President, Publishing Group: Christopher M. Little

Vice President, Consumer Marketing & Development: Hal Oringer

Meredith Corporation

Chairman and Chief Executive Officer: William T. Kerr

Chairman of the Executive Committee: E. T. Meredith III

All of us at Better Homes and Gardens® Books are dedicated to providing you with the information and ideas you need to create delicious foods. We welcome your comments and suggestions. Write to us at: Better Homes and Gardens Books, Cookbook Editorial Department, 1716 Locust St., Des Moines, Iowa 50309-3023.

Our seal assures you that every recipe in *Low-Fat Bold Flavors* has been tested in the Better Homes and Gardens® Test Kitchen. This means that each recipe is practical and reliable, and meets our high standards of taste appeal. We guarantee your satisfaction with this book for as long as you own it.

Cover photo: Chicken, Long Beans, & Tomato Stir-Fry *(see recipe, page 63)*

Better Homes and Gardens.

Low-Fat Bold Flavors

Contents

Everywhere you turn low-fat dishes abound, but none are as exciting or full-flavored as the ones you'll discover in *Low-Fat Bold Flavors*. This cookbook—with 80 family-style entrées and desserts—will inspire you to get busy in the kitchen. Each easy-on-the-cook idea is pictured in full color and features only the best ingredients teamed with spunky spices and flavorful herbs. What's more, each recipe is accompanied by nutrition facts that highlight the amount of fat, the percent of Daily Value of fat, and exchanges based on the system used by the American Diabetes Association. Try any of these dynamite recipes and you'll be convinced low fat never tasted better!

Beef,
Pork & Lamb

Garlic-Sage-Marinated
Beef Pot Roast
See Recipe, Page 8

Lean meat and a handful of flavorful ingredients mean great low-fat dining tonight.

Herbed Beef Tenderloin

Indirect grilling allows roasts to cook slowly so they will be tender and juicy when done. Buy an inexpensive foil pan at the grocery store to use as a drip pan. The size will depend on your grill.

Total Fat:	**9 g**
Daily Value Fat:	**14%**
Saturated Fat:	**3 g**
Daily Value Saturated Fat:	**15%**

Nutrition Facts
Per Serving:
Calories	189
Total Fat	9 g
Saturated Fat	3 g
Cholesterol	66 mg
Sodium	193 mg
Carbohydrate	3 g
Fiber	0 g
Protein	23 g

Exchanges:
3 Lean Meat

¼ cup finely snipped fresh parsley	1 teaspoon olive oil or cooking oil
2 tablespoons Dijon-style mustard	½ teaspoon coarsely ground black pepper
1 tablespoon snipped fresh rosemary	1 2-pound beef tenderloin roast, trimmed of separable fat
2 teaspoons snipped fresh thyme	½ cup light dairy sour cream
2 cloves garlic, minced	2 teaspoons Dijon-style mustard

In small mixing bowl stir together parsley, the 2 tablespoons mustard, the rosemary, thyme, garlic, oil, and pepper. Rub over top and sides of meat.

In a covered grill arrange hot coals around a drip pan. Test for medium-hot heat above the drip pan.* Place roast on grill rack over drip pan, but not over coals. Insert a meat thermometer in center of roast. Lower the grill hood. Grill about 45 minutes or until thermometer registers 140°. (Or, place on a rack in a shallow roasting pan. Insert a meat thermometer into center of meat. Roast, uncovered, in a 325° oven for 30 to 45 minutes or until thermometer registers 140°.)

Cover meat with foil and let stand for 15 minutes (the temperature of the meat will rise 5° during standing).

Meanwhile, stir together sour cream and the 2 teaspoons mustard. Thinly slice meat. Serve with sour cream mixture. If desired, sprinkle with additional black pepper. Makes 8 servings.

*Note: To check for medium-hot heat, hold your hand, palm side down, over where the meat will cook and at about the same height of the meat. The heat is right when you can hold your hand there for only 3 seconds.

Prep time: 5 minutes   **Grilling time:** 45 minutes   **Standing time:** 15 minutes

Beef with Mushroom-Tomato Sauce

For a more elegant dinner, grill beef tenderloin instead of eye of round steaks and make the sauce using ⅓ cup dry red wine plus ⅓ cup water in place of the vegetable juice.

Total Fat:	**8 g**
Daily Value Fat:	**12%**
Saturated Fat:	**2 g**
Daily Value Saturated Fat:	**10%**

Nutrition Facts
Per Serving:

Calories	173
Total Fat	8 g
Saturated Fat	2 g
Cholesterol	58 mg
Sodium	172 mg
Carbohydrate	5 g
Fiber	0 g
Protein	20 g

Exchanges:
3 Lean Meat
1 Vegetable

⅛ teaspoon pepper
4 3-ounce beef eye of round
  steaks, trimmed of
  separable fat
1 cup sliced fresh mushrooms
½ cup sliced green onions

2 cloves garlic, minced
2 teaspoons margarine or butter
2 teaspoons cornstarch
⅔ cup low-sodium vegetable juice
½ teaspoon instant beef bouillon
  granules

Rub pepper over meat. Grill steaks on the rack of an uncovered grill directly over medium coals until desired doneness, turning once. (Allow 8 to 12 minutes for medium rare or 12 to 15 minutes for medium.)

Meanwhile, in a saucepan cook mushrooms, onions, and garlic in hot margarine or butter until vegetables are tender. Stir in cornstarch. Add vegetable juice and beef bouillon granules. Cook and stir until thickened and bubbly. Cook and stir for 2 minutes more. Keep warm while cooking meat. Serve the sauce over meat. Makes 4 servings.

Broiling Directions: Place the meat on the unheated rack of a broiler pan. Broil 4 to 5 inches from the heat until desired doneness, turning once. (Allow 10 to 12 minutes for medium rare or 12 to 15 minutes for medium.)

Prep time: 20 minutes   **Grilling time:** 8 minutes

Garlic-Sage-Marinated Beef Pot Roast

Red wine, tomato paste, and garlic give this fork-tender roast a robust, well-rounded flavor. (Also pictured on pages 4–5.)

1	2- to 2½-pound boneless beef chuck pot roast
¾	cup dry red wine or tomato juice
2	tablespoons tomato paste
1	tablespoon snipped fresh sage or ½ teaspoon ground sage
2	teaspoons instant beef bouillon granules
¼	teaspoon pepper
10	cloves garlic, halved
1	tablespoon cooking oil
1¼	pounds whole tiny new potatoes or 4 medium potatoes
4	medium carrots, cut into 2-inch pieces
2	small onions, cut into wedges
2	stalks celery, bias-sliced into 1-inch pieces
½	cup cold water
¼	cup all-purpose flour

Trim fat from roast; place meat in a heavy plastic bag set in a bowl. Combine the wine or tomato juice, tomato paste, sage, bouillon granules, pepper, and garlic. Pour over meat. Close bag and marinate in refrigerator for 6 to 24 hours, turning occasionally. Remove meat from marinade, reserving marinade.

In a kettle or pot, brown the roast on both sides in hot oil. Drain well. Pour reserved marinade over roast. Bring to boiling; reduce heat. Cover and simmer for 1 hour.

Remove a narrow strip of peel from around the center of each new potato. (Or, peel and quarter each medium potato.) Add potatoes, carrots, onions, and celery to meat. Cover and simmer 45 to 60 minutes or until tender, adding some water if necessary. Transfer meat and vegetables to a serving platter; cover to keep warm while preparing gravy.

For gravy, measure pan juices; skim fat. If necessary, add water to equal 1¾ cups liquid; return to pan. Combine the ½ cup cold water and the flour. Stir into juices. Cook and stir until bubbly. Cook and stir for 1 minute more. Season with salt and pepper. Serve with meat and vegetables. If desired, garnish with additional fresh sage. Makes 8 servings.

Prep time: 30 minutes   **Marinating time:** 6 hours   **Cooking time:** 1¾ hours

Beef Saté with Peanut Sauce

Saté (sah-TAY), an Indonesian dish, typically is skewered meat, poultry, or seafood served with a peanut sauce. It can be served as an appetizer. As a main dish, serve with pasta and grilled vegetables.

1 pound lean boneless beef sirloin steak, cut 1 inch thick and trimmed of separable fat
1 small onion, cut up
2 tablespoons reduced-sodium soy sauce
2 tablespoons lime juice
1 teaspoon sugar
1 teaspoon ground cumin
1 clove garlic, minced

¼ cup reduced-sodium chicken broth
2 tablespoons peanut butter
1 tablespoon molasses or honey
1 teaspoon reduced-sodium soy sauce
¼ to ½ teaspoon crushed red pepper
1 clove garlic, minced

Cut beef into 1¼-inch pieces. Place in a plastic bag set in a deep bowl.

For marinade, in a food processor bowl or blender container place onion, the 2 tablespoons soy sauce, the lime juice, sugar, cumin, and 1 clove garlic. Cover; process or blend until smooth. Pour over meat in bag; close bag. Marinate meat in the refrigerator about 4 hours, turning bag occasionally.

For sauce, in a saucepan gradually stir broth into peanut butter. Stir in molasses or honey, the 1 teaspoon soy sauce, crushed red pepper, and 1 clove garlic. Cook and stir until heated through. Keep warm.

Drain meat, discarding marinade. Thread meat onto 4 skewers, leaving ¼-inch space between pieces. Arrange skewers on the unheated rack of a broiler pan. Broil 3 to 4 inches from the heat for 7 to 9 minutes or until desired doneness, turning occasionally to brown evenly. Serve sauce with meat for dipping. Makes 4 servings.

Total Fat:	14 g
Daily Value Fat:	22%
Saturated Fat:	5 g
Daily Value Saturated Fat:	25%

Nutrition Facts
Per Serving:

Calories	274
Total Fat	14 g
Saturated Fat	5 g
Cholesterol	76 mg
Sodium	313 mg
Carbohydrate	7 g
Fiber	1 g
Protein	29 g

Exchanges:
4 Medium-Fat Meat
1 Vegetable
½ Fat

Prep time: 20 minutes   **Marinating time:** 4 hours   **Broiling time:** 7 minutes

Citrus-Tequila Fajitas

Scoring and marinating tenderizes flank steak, a naturally lean cut of meat, without chemical tenderizers.

12 ounces beef flank steak
3 tablespoons frozen orange juice concentrate, thawed
3 tablespoons tequila or water
2 tablespoons lime juice
1 teaspoon grated fresh ginger
½ teaspoon dried oregano, crushed
⅛ teaspoon salt
⅛ teaspoon ground red pepper

1 clove garlic, minced
8 small corn or four 8- to 10-inch flour tortillas
½ cup red and/or yellow sweet pepper strips
½ of a small onion, sliced and separated into rings
Sliced fresh chili peppers (optional)

Score meat by making shallow cuts at 1-inch intervals diagonally across steak in a diamond pattern. Repeat on the other side. Place meat in a plastic bag set in a shallow dish. For marinade, mix juice concentrate, tequila or water, lime juice, ginger, oregano, salt, ground red pepper, and garlic. Pour over meat. Close bag. Marinate 30 minutes at room temperature or in the refrigerator up to 4 hours, turning bag occasionally.

Drain meat, reserving marinade. Place meat on the unheated rack of a broiler pan. Broil 3 inches from the heat for 12 to 14 minutes or until desired doneness, turning once. (Or, grill meat on the rack of an uncovered grill directly over medium coals for 12 to 14 minutes or until desired doneness, turning once.) Thinly slice meat diagonally across the grain.

To warm tortillas, wrap in foil. Place beside the broiler pan or on grill rack for the last 8 minutes of cooking meat. Meanwhile, pour reserved marinade into a small saucepan. Stir in sweet pepper strips and onion. Bring to boiling; reduce heat. Simmer, uncovered, for 3 to 5 minutes or until vegetables are tender.

To serve, fill tortillas with beef. Using a slotted spoon, spoon pepper mixture over beef. If desired, sprinkle with chili peppers. Roll up fajitas. Makes 4 servings.

Prep time: 10 minutes **Marinating time:** 30 minutes **Broiling time:** 12 minutes

Beef Paprika With Noodles

Using fat-free yogurt or sour cream in this dish gives the creamy richness that is traditional yet keeps the fat grams in check.

1	pound boneless beef sirloin steak, trimmed of separable fat	1½	teaspoons instant beef bouillon granules
	Nonstick spray coating	¼	teaspoon pepper
2	teaspoons cooking oil	½	cup plain fat-free yogurt or fat-free dairy sour cream
3	cups sliced fresh mushrooms	2	tablespoons all-purpose flour
1	medium onion, sliced and separated into rings	3	cups hot cooked curly noodles or brown rice
1	clove garlic, minced	2	tablespoons snipped fresh parsley
1⅓	cups water		
1	tablespoon paprika		

Partially freeze meat about 30 minutes. Thinly slice across the grain into bite-size strips. Spray an unheated large skillet with nonstick coating. Preheat over medium-high heat. Quickly brown beef, half at a time, in skillet. Remove all meat from skillet. Add oil to skillet. Cook mushrooms, onion, and garlic in hot oil until mushrooms are tender.

Add the water, paprika, bouillon granules, and pepper to the skillet. Return meat to the skillet. Bring to boiling; reduce heat. Simmer, covered, about 15 minutes or until meat is tender. Stir together yogurt or sour cream and flour. Add to mixture in skillet. Cook and stir until thickened and bubbly. Cook and stir for 1 minute more.

Toss together hot noodles or rice and parsley. Serve meat mixture on the noodle or rice mixture. Makes 6 servings.

Prep time: 50 minutes   **Cooking time:** 15 minutes

Spicy Beef and Bean Burgers

Using beans to replace some of the ground meat in recipes has many nutritional benefits. They add protein, fiber, and carbohydrates without adding fat or cholesterol.

1 slightly beaten egg white
½ of a 15-ounce can (¾ cup) pinto beans, drained and mashed
¼ cup soft whole wheat bread crumbs
¼ cup finely chopped celery
1 tablespoon canned diced green chili peppers or 1 teaspoon chopped canned jalapeño peppers
⅛ teaspoon garlic powder
1 pound lean ground beef
8 lettuce leaves
4 7-inch flour tortillas, halved
1 cup salsa

In a large mixing bowl combine egg white, beans, bread crumbs, celery, chili peppers, and garlic powder. Add ground beef; mix well.

Shape meat mixture into eight ½-inch-thick oval patties. Place the patties on the unheated rack of a broiler pan. Broil 4 inches from the heat for 12 to 14 minutes or until no longer pink, turning once.

To serve, place a lettuce leaf and a burger in the center of each tortilla half. Top burger with 1 tablespoon of the salsa. Bring ends of tortilla up and over burger. Top with another tablespoon salsa. Makes 8 servings.

Total Fat:	8 g
Daily Value Fat:	12%
Saturated Fat:	2 g
Daily Value Saturated Fat:	10%

Nutrition Facts
Per Serving:

Calories	185
Total Fat	8 g
Saturated Fat	2 g
Cholesterol	36 mg
Sodium	339 mg
Carbohydrate	16 g
Fiber	2 g
Protein	14 g

Exchanges:
1 Starch
2 Meat

Prep time: 15 minutes **Broiling time:** 12 minutes

Spaghetti Squash with Chili

You can afford a generous serving of this delicious chili-flavored meat sauce ladled over low-calorie spaghetti squash. If you don't have time to make the squash, serve the chili over spaghetti.

1	2½- to 3-pound spaghetti squash	2	teaspoons chili powder
12	ounces lean ground beef	1	teaspoon snipped fresh oregano or ½ teaspoon dried oregano, crushed
½	cup chopped onion		
1	clove garlic, minced		
½	teaspoon cornstarch	½	cup shredded Monterey Jack cheese (2 ounces) (optional)
1	8-ounce can low-sodium tomato sauce		Sliced fresh chili peppers (optional)
⅔	cup tomato juice		
1	11-ounce can whole kernel corn with sweet peppers, drained		

Halve the spaghetti squash lengthwise and remove seeds. Place, cut sides down, on a baking sheet. Bake in a 350° oven for 45 to 50 minutes or until tender. Using a fork, shred and separate the spaghetti squash into strands.

Meanwhile, for sauce, in a large skillet cook beef, onion, and garlic until meat is brown and onion is tender. Drain off fat.

Stir in cornstarch. Add tomato sauce and tomato juice. Stir in corn, chili powder, and oregano. Cook and stir until slightly thickened and bubbly. Cook and stir 2 minutes more.

To serve, spoon the meat mixture over spaghetti squash. If desired, top with Monterey Jack cheese and garnish with chili peppers and additional fresh oregano. Makes 4 servings.

Microwave Directions: Place squash halves, cut sides down, in a microwave-safe baking dish with ¼ cup water. Cover and microwave on 100% power (high) for 15 to 20 minutes or until tender, rearranging once. Continue as above.

Prep time: 20 minutes **Baking time:** 45 minutes

Lasagna

By using lower-fat cheeses in this recipe, we slashed the fat per serving in half. This slimmer version also has 75 fewer calories than a standard lasagna recipe.

Total Fat:	8 g
Daily Value Fat:	12%
Saturated Fat:	5 g
Daily Value Saturated Fat:	25%

Nutrition Facts
Per Serving:

Calories	281
Total Fat	8 g
Saturated Fat	5 g
Cholesterol	60 mg
Sodium	491 mg
Carbohydrate	27 g
Fiber	2 g
Protein	23 g

Exchanges:
1½ Starch
2 Lean Meat
1 Vegetable

8 ounces lean ground beef
1 cup chopped onion
2 cloves garlic, minced
1 16-ounce can low-sodium tomatoes, undrained and cut up
1 6-ounce can low-sodium tomato paste
1½ teaspoons dried basil, crushed
1½ teaspoons dried oregano, crushed
1 teaspoon fennel seed, crushed
¼ teaspoon salt
9 packaged dried lasagna noodles
1 12-ounce carton low-fat cottage cheese, drained
1½ cups shredded reduced-fat mozzarella cheese (6 ounces)
¼ cup grated Parmesan cheese (1 ounce)
1 egg
2 tablespoons snipped fresh parsley

In a saucepan cook beef, onion, and garlic until meat is brown. Drain off fat. Stir in undrained tomatoes, tomato paste, basil, oregano, fennel seed, and salt. Bring to boiling; reduce heat. Simmer, covered, for 15 minutes, stirring occasionally.

Meanwhile, cook lasagna noodles according to package directions. Drain; rinse with cold water. Drain well.

For filling, combine cottage cheese, 1 cup of the mozzarella cheese, the Parmesan cheese, egg, parsley, and ¼ teaspoon pepper.

Layer one-third of the cooked noodles in a 2-quart rectangular baking dish, trimming ends to fit. Spread with half of the filling. Top with one-third of sauce. Repeat layers. Top with remaining noodles and sauce. Sprinkle with remaining mozzarella.

Bake, uncovered, in a 375° oven for 30 to 35 minutes or until heated through. Let stand 10 minutes before serving. Makes 8 servings.

Prep time: 45 minutes   **Baking time:** 30 minutes   **Standing time:** 10 minutes

Osso Buco

Using several dried seasonings simplifies this variation of classic osso buco—braised veal shanks prepared with wine and tomatoes.

2 to 2½ pounds veal shanks, cut into 2½-inch pieces
Lemon-pepper seasoning
Salt
2 tablespoons all-purpose flour
2 tablespoons cooking oil
1 14½-ounce can tomatoes, undrained and cut up
1 cup chopped onion
½ cup water
¼ cup dry white wine or chicken broth
2 tablespoons mixed vegetable flakes
½ teaspoon instant beef bouillon granules
½ teaspoon dried Italian seasoning, crushed
¼ teaspoon dried finely shredded orange peel
⅛ teaspoon dried minced garlic
Dash pepper
2 to 3 cups hot cooked rice
1 tablespoon snipped fresh parsley or 1 teaspoon dried parsley flakes
½ cup shredded carrot (optional)

Sprinkle veal with lemon-pepper seasoning and salt. Coat lightly with flour; shake off excess.

In a kettle brown veal in hot oil. Drain well. Add the undrained tomatoes, onion, water, wine or broth, vegetable flakes, bouillon granules, Italian seasoning, orange peel, garlic, and pepper. Bring to boiling; reduce heat. Cover and simmer 50 to 60 minutes or until tender.

Remove meat from kettle; cut meat from bones. Transfer meat to a serving platter. Cover and keep warm. Boil broth mixture gently, uncovered, about 10 minutes or until of desired consistency. To serve, toss rice with parsley and, if desired, shredded carrot. Place meat on rice. Spoon some broth mixture over meat. Pass remaining broth mixture. If desired, garnish with additional fresh parsley. Makes 6 servings.

Prep time: 15 minutes   **Cooking time:** 1 hour

Mustard-Orange Pork Tenderloin

A mixture of vegetables, such as cut-up red onions, baby carrots, and chunks of zucchini, can be roasted alongside the meat. Just spray the vegetables with olive oil-flavored nonstick coating before placing them in the pan around the meat.

Nutrition Facts

Total Fat:	**4 g**
Daily Value Fat:	**6%**
Saturated Fat:	**1 g**
Daily Value Saturated Fat:	**5%**

Nutrition Facts
Per Serving:

Calories	240
Total Fat	4 g
Saturated Fat	1 g
Cholesterol	60 mg
Sodium	334 mg
Carbohydrate	32 g
Fiber	3 g
Protein	21 g

Exchanges:
3 Meat
½ Vegetable
2 Fruit

12 ounces pork tenderloin
½ cup apricot preserves or orange marmalade
3 tablespoons Dijon-style mustard
Nonstick spray coating

2 cups sliced fresh mushrooms
½ cup sliced green onions
2 tablespoons orange juice

Trim any fat from meat. Place in a shallow roasting pan. Insert a meat thermometer. Roast, uncovered, in a 425° oven for 10 minutes.

Meanwhile, in a small mixing bowl stir together preserves and mustard. Spoon half of the mustard mixture over the tenderloin; set remaining mixture aside. Roast for 15 to 25 minutes more or until thermometer registers 160°. Cover meat with foil and let stand for 5 minutes before carving.

Spray a medium saucepan with nonstick coating. Add mushrooms and onions. Cook and stir for 2 to 3 minutes or until mushrooms are tender. Stir in remaining mustard mixture and orange juice. Cook and stir until heated through. To serve, thinly slice roast. Spoon mushroom mixture over roast. Makes 4 servings.

Prep time: 10 minutes   **Roasting time:** 25 minutes

Pork Chops With Italian Vegetables

Cook the vegetables in a skillet while the chops are broiling. Fresh basil and oregano add the Italian touch.

1 tablespoon frozen orange juice concentrate, thawed
1 clove garlic, minced
⅛ teaspoon black pepper
4 boneless pork loin chops, cut ½ inch thick and trimmed of separable fat (about 1¼ pounds total)
  Nonstick spray coating
2 medium zucchini and/or yellow summer squash, cut into thin strips

1 small red or green sweet pepper, cut into strips
1 small onion, sliced
2 teaspoons snipped fresh basil or ¾ teaspoon dried basil, crushed
1 teaspoon snipped fresh oregano or ½ teaspoon dried oregano, crushed
⅛ teaspoon salt
8 cherry tomatoes, halved

Combine orange juice concentrate, garlic, and black pepper. Set aside.

Place chops on the unheated rack of a broiler pan. Broil 3 to 4 inches from the heat for 5 minutes. Brush with orange juice mixture. Turn and broil about 5 minutes more or until chops are just slightly pink in center and juices run clear. Brush with remaining orange juice mixture.

Meanwhile, spray an unheated large skillet with nonstick coating. Add zucchini, sweet pepper, onion, dried basil (if using), dried oregano (if using), and salt. Cook and stir over medium-high heat about 4 minutes or until vegetables are crisp-tender. Stir in tomato halves and fresh basil and oregano (if using). Reduce heat; cover and cook for 1 minute more. Serve vegetables with pork chops. If desired, garnish with additional fresh basil. Makes 4 servings.

Start to finish: 30 minutes

Barbecued Pork Sandwiches

Making your own barbecue sauce, rather than using a commercial sauce, reduces the sodium content in this recipe by almost half.

Total Fat:	**5 g**
Daily Value Fat:	**8%**
Saturated Fat:	**2 g**
Daily Value Saturated Fat:	**10%**

Nutrition Facts
Per Serving:

Calories	255
Total Fat	5 g
Saturated Fat	2 g
Cholesterol	60 mg
Sodium	305 mg
Carbohydrate	30 g
Fiber	2 g
Protein	24 g

Exchanges:
2 Starch
2½ Meat

Nonstick spray coating
1 medium onion, chopped (½ cup)
2 cloves garlic, minced
½ cup water
½ of a 6-ounce can (⅓ cup) tomato paste
¼ cup red wine vinegar
1 tablespoon brown sugar
1½ teaspoons chili powder
1 teaspoon dried oregano, crushed
1 teaspoon Worcestershire sauce
12 ounces pork tenderloin
1 medium green pepper, chopped (¾ cup)
4 whole wheat buns, split and toasted

For sauce, spray a small saucepan with nonstick coating. Cook onion and garlic in the saucepan until tender. Stir in water, tomato paste, vinegar, brown sugar, chili powder, oregano, and Worcestershire sauce. Bring to boiling; reduce heat. Simmer, uncovered, about 20 minutes or until desired consistency, stirring occasionally.

Meanwhile, trim any fat from meat. Cut into bite-size strips. Spray a large skillet with nonstick coating. Add pork to skillet. Cook and stir pork over medium-high heat for 2 to 3 minutes or until juices run clear. Stir in green pepper and sauce. Heat through. Spoon mixture onto bottoms of buns. Cover with tops. Makes 4 servings.

Prep time: 20 minutes   **Cooking time:** 20 minutes

Pork and Eggplant Stew

If you sprinkle bowls of this Mediterranean-style stew with the optional feta cheese, add only 19 calories and 2 grams fat to the nutrition facts per serving. The small addition is worth it.

Nonstick spray coating
8 ounces lean boneless pork, cut into ¾-inch cubes
1 large onion, sliced and separated into rings
1 clove garlic, minced
1 small eggplant, peeled and cubed (4 cups)
1 14½-ounce can low-sodium tomatoes, undrained and cut up
1 medium green pepper, cut into strips
1 5½-ounce can low-sodium vegetable juice
1 teaspoon dried oregano, crushed
1 teaspoon dried basil, crushed
¼ teaspoon salt
¼ teaspoon black pepper
2 tablespoons snipped fresh parsley
¼ cup crumbled feta cheese (optional)

Spray a Dutch oven with nonstick coating. Add pork, onion, and garlic; cook over medium heat until pork is brown and onion is tender.

Stir in eggplant, undrained tomatoes, green pepper, vegetable juice, oregano, basil, salt, and black pepper.

Bring to boiling; reduce heat. Simmer, covered, for 10 to 15 minutes or until vegetables are tender. Stir in parsley.

Divide the stew among 4 soup bowls. If desired, sprinkle each serving with feta cheese. Makes 4 servings.

Prep time: 30 minutes   **Cooking time:** 10 minutes

Pork and Fruit Salad

Pork tenderloin has only 4 grams of fat and 67 mg of cholesterol in a 3-ounce serving. That's similar to skinless chicken breast, which has 3 grams fat and 72 mg cholesterol in a 3-ounce serving.

¼ cup fat-free mayonnaise dressing or salad dressing
¼ cup unsweetened pineapple juice or orange juice
1 tablespoon honey mustard
½ teaspoon grated fresh ginger
12 ounces pork tenderloin
2 tablespoons honey mustard
6 cups torn spinach and/or romaine lettuce

2 cups sliced pears, nectarines, apples, and/or peeled peaches
12 small clusters champagne grapes
Coarsely ground pepper (optional)

For dressing, in a small mixing bowl stir together the mayonnaise dressing or salad dressing, pineapple or orange juice, the 1 tablespoon honey mustard, and the ginger. Cover and refrigerate until serving time.

Trim any fat from the tenderloin. Place in a shallow roasting pan. Insert a meat thermometer. Roast, uncovered, in a 425° oven for 20 minutes.

Spoon the 2 tablespoons honey mustard over the tenderloin. Roast for 5 to 10 minutes more or until thermometer registers 160°. Cover meat loosely with foil and let stand for 5 minutes before carving.

Meanwhile, arrange greens, fruit slices, and grapes on 4 salad plates. To serve, thinly slice pork roast. Top salads with pork slices. Stir dressing. Drizzle dressing over salads. If desired, sprinkle with pepper. Makes 4 servings.

Total Fat:	**4 g**
Daily Value Fat:	**6%**
Saturated Fat:	**1 g**
Daily Value Saturated Fat:	**5%**

Nutrition Facts
Per Serving:

Calories	228
Total Fat	4 g
Saturated Fat	1 g
Cholesterol	60 mg
Sodium	442 mg
Carbohydrate	27 g
Fiber	5 g
Protein	22 g

Exchanges:
2½ Lean Meat
1½ Vegetable
1 Fruit

Prep time: 15 minutes   **Roasting time:** 25 minutes   **Standing time:** 5 minutes

Sweet-and-Sour Ham Balls

While the meatballs bake, cook the vegetables, pineapple, and sauce on top of the stove. Use a gentle hand when stirring the ham balls into the sauce so they retain their shape.

1 beaten egg	½ cup reduced-sodium chicken broth
1 cup bran flakes	¼ cup red wine vinegar
⅓ cup fat-free milk	2 tablespoons cornstarch
1 teaspoon grated fresh ginger or ¼ teaspoon ground ginger	2 tablespoons honey
8 ounces ground veal or lean ground beef	2 tablespoons reduced-sodium soy sauce
8 ounces ground cooked ham	1 cup fresh or frozen pea pods
1 15¼-ounce can pineapple chunks (juice-packed)	3 cups hot cooked rice
1½ cups thinly sliced carrots	

In a large bowl combine egg, bran flakes, milk, and ginger. Let stand 5 minutes. Add veal or beef and ham; mix well. Shape into 24 meatballs.

Arrange meatballs in a 2-quart rectangular baking dish. Bake, uncovered, in a 350° oven for 30 minutes. Spoon off fat.

Meanwhile, for sauce, drain pineapple, reserving juice. Set both aside. In a large covered saucepan cook carrots in broth about 5 minutes or just until tender. Do not drain.

Combine vinegar, cornstarch, honey, and soy sauce. Stir into carrot mixture. Stir in reserved pineapple juice. Cook and stir until thickened and bubbly. Stir in pea pods; cook 2 minutes more. Stir in pineapple; heat through. Add meatballs; stir gently to coat. Serve with rice. Makes 6 servings.

Start to finish: 50 minutes

Total Fat:	**5 g**
Daily Value Fat:	**8%**
Saturated Fat:	**2 g**
Daily Value Saturated Fat:	**10%**

Nutrition Facts
Per Serving:

Calories	345
Total Fat	5 g
Saturated Fat	2 g
Cholesterol	86 mg
Sodium	819 mg
Carbohydrate	54 g
Fiber	4 g
Protein	23 g

Exchanges:
2 Starch
2 Lean Meat
1 Vegetable
1 Fruit

Lamb Chops With Sweet Pepper and Onion

The lamb chops also can be grilled directly over medium coals. Grill for 10 to 14 minutes for medium rare or 14 to 16 minutes for medium doneness.

4 lamb loin chops, trimmed of separable fat (about 12 ounces total)
1 medium onion, thinly sliced
1 cup red and/or yellow sweet pepper strips
2 cloves garlic, minced

2 tablespoons snipped fresh herbs (such as basil, oregano, thyme, and/or marjoram) or 1 teaspoon dried herb or mixture of herbs, crushed
2 teaspoons cooking oil
2 tablespoons red or white wine vinegar
4 teaspoons brown sugar

Place the lamb chops on the unheated rack of a broiler pan. Broil 3 to 4 inches from the heat for 7 to 11 minutes for medium doneness, turning once.

Meanwhile, in a covered large skillet cook onion, sweet pepper, garlic, and dried herb (if using) in hot oil until vegetables are just tender, stirring once. Stir in vinegar, brown sugar, and fresh herb (if using); heat through.

To serve, spoon onion mixture over lamb chops. If desired, garnish with additional fresh herb. Makes 4 servings.

Start to finish: 12 minutes

Nutrition Facts

Total Fat:	10 g
Daily Value Fat:	15%
Saturated Fat:	3 g
Daily Value Saturated Fat:	15%

Nutrition Facts
Per Serving:

Calories	182
Total Fat	10 g
Saturated Fat	3 g
Cholesterol	52 mg
Sodium	51 mg
Carbohydrate	7 g
Fiber	0 g
Protein	16 g

Exchanges:
2 Lean Meat
1 Vegetable
½ Fat

Curried Lamb With Apricot Rice

Different brands of curry powder use varying proportions of as many as 20 ground spices, making some hotter than others. Experiment with different brands to see which you like best.

Total Fat:	**12 g**
Daily Value Fat:	**18%**
Saturated Fat:	**3 g**
Daily Value Saturated Fat:	**15%**

Nutrition Facts
Per Serving:

Calories	381
Total Fat	12 g
Saturated Fat	3 g
Cholesterol	55 mg
Sodium	352 mg
Carbohydrate	47 g
Fiber	4 g
Protein	22 g

Exchanges:
2 Starch
2 Medium-Fat Meat
1 Fruit

1	pound lean boneless lamb, trimmed of separable fat
1	tablespoon cooking oil
1	medium onion, chopped
1	stalk celery, sliced
1	clove garlic, minced
2 to 3	teaspoons curry powder
1	14½-ounce can reduced-sodium chicken broth
½	cup water
1	cup uncooked brown rice
⅓	cup snipped dried apricots
½	teaspoon sugar
⅛	teaspoon ground cloves

Cut meat into ¾-inch cubes. In large saucepan brown half the meat in the hot oil. Remove from saucepan.

Brown the remaining meat with the onion, celery, and garlic until onion is tender. Return all of the meat to saucepan; stir in curry powder. Cook for 1 minute more. Remove from heat.

In a 2-quart casserole combine chicken broth and water. Stir in rice, apricots, sugar, and cloves. Add browned meat mixture. Bake, covered, in a 350° oven for 1¼ to 1½ hours or until meat is tender and rice is done. Makes 4 servings.

Prep time: 30 minutes   **Baking time:** 1¼ hours

Chicken & Turkey

Chicken with
Artichokes
See Recipe, Page 28

Sometimes **exotic,**
sometimes **home-style,**
these **anything-but-ordinary**
poultry ideas make first-rate,
low-fat choices for healthy meals.

Grilled Jerk Chicken

Jamaican jerk seasoning is a dry blend of chilies, thyme, and spices (such as cinnamon, ginger, cloves, and allspice). Use as a rub or combined with a liquid for a marinade, as it is here.

4 medium skinless, boneless chicken breast halves (about 1 pound total)
1 large onion, quartered
1 to 2 jalapeño peppers, seeded and cut up*
1 tablespoon snipped fresh thyme or 1 teaspoon dried thyme, crushed
½ teaspoon ground allspice
¼ teaspoon salt
¼ teaspoon ground nutmeg
Dash ground cloves
¼ cup orange juice
Torn mixed greens (optional)
Pineapple wedges (optional)
Orange slices, quartered (optional)

Rinse chicken; pat dry with paper towels. Place chicken in a plastic bag set in a shallow dish.

In a food processor bowl or blender container combine onion, jalapeño peppers, thyme, allspice, salt, nutmeg, and cloves. Cover; process or blend until almost smooth. With food processor or blender running, add the orange juice. Process or blend until almost smooth. Pour over chicken. Close bag. Marinate in the refrigerator for at least 4 hours or up to 24 hours, turning occasionally.

Drain chicken; discard marinade. Grill chicken on the rack of an uncovered grill directly over medium coals for 12 to 15 minutes or until tender and no longer pink, turning once. If desired, place greens on plates with pineapple and oranges. Add chicken. If desired, drizzle with additional orange juice. Makes 4 servings.

*Note: Because chili peppers, such as jalapeños, contain volatile oils that can burn your skin and eyes, avoid direct contact with them as much as possible. When working with chili peppers, wear plastic gloves. If your bare hands touch the chili peppers, wash your hands well with soap and water.

Prep time: 15 minutes   **Marinating time:** 4 hours   **Grilling time:** 12 minutes

Chicken Cacciatore

Cacciatore is Italian for "hunter," and usually contains mushrooms, onions, tomatoes, and herbs. If you like, replace the ¼ cup water with red wine, an optional ingredient often used in this classic dish.

4 small skinless, boneless chicken breast halves (about 12 ounces total)
   Nonstick spray coating
1 14½-ounce can stewed tomatoes, undrained
1 medium green pepper, cut into thin strips
½ cup sliced fresh mushrooms
¼ cup chopped onion
¼ cup water or dry red wine
2 teaspoons dried Italian seasoning, crushed
⅛ teaspoon black pepper

Rinse chicken; pat dry with paper towels. Spray an unheated large skillet with nonstick coating. Preheat over medium heat. Add chicken and cook about 6 minutes or until lightly browned, turning to brown evenly.

Stir in stewed tomatoes, green pepper, mushrooms, onion, water or wine, Italian seasoning, and black pepper. Bring to boiling; reduce heat. Simmer, covered, about 15 minutes or until chicken is tender and no longer pink. Remove chicken from skillet; cover chicken to keep warm. Simmer tomato mixture, uncovered, about 5 minutes or to desired consistency. Makes 4 servings.

Nutrition Facts

Total Fat:	3 g
Daily Value Fat:	5%
Saturated Fat:	1 g
Daily Value Saturated Fat:	5%

Nutrition Facts
Per Serving:

Calories	134
Total Fat	3 g
Saturated Fat	1 g
Cholesterol	45 mg
Sodium	309 mg
Carbohydrate	10 g
Fiber	3 g
Protein	18 g

Exchanges:
2 Lean Meat
2 Vegetable

Prep time: 25 minutes   **Cooking time:** 20 minutes

Chicken with Artichokes

Using frozen artichokes in this wholesome Italian-style dish is convenient because all inedible parts are already removed. (Also pictured on pages 24–25.)

1½ pounds meaty chicken pieces (breasts, thighs, and drumsticks), skinned
¼ teaspoon salt
⅛ teaspoon pepper
½ cup dried tomatoes (not oil-packed)
2 cups sliced fresh mushrooms
1 large leek, thinly sliced, or ⅓ cup chopped onion
2 cloves garlic, minced
½ teaspoon dried rosemary, crushed, or 2 teaspoons snipped fresh rosemary
2 tablespoons olive oil
¾ cup chicken broth
1 teaspoon finely shredded lemon peel
3 tablespoons lemon juice
1 8- or 9-ounce package frozen artichoke hearts

Rinse chicken; pat dry with paper towels. Sprinkle chicken pieces with salt and pepper. Using scissors, cut dried tomatoes into thin strips. Set aside.

In a large skillet cook mushrooms, leek or onion, garlic, and dried rosemary (if using) in hot oil until leek is tender. Remove with slotted spoon; set aside. Add chicken pieces to the skillet and cook over medium heat for 10 minutes, turning to brown evenly. Add tomatoes, leek mixture, broth, lemon peel, and lemon juice to the skillet. Bring to boiling; reduce heat. Cover and simmer for 20 minutes.

Meanwhile, thaw artichoke hearts under cold water just enough to separate them. Drain. Halve any large artichokes. Add to skillet along with fresh rosemary (if using). Return to boiling; reduce heat. Cover and simmer for 10 to 15 minutes or until chicken is tender and no longer pink. To serve, transfer chicken and vegetables to a serving platter. If desired, garnish with lemon wedges and additional fresh rosemary. Makes 4 servings.

Prep time: 20 minutes **Cooking time:** 45 minutes

Nutrition Facts

Total Fat:	13 g
Daily Value Fat:	19%
Saturated Fat:	3 g
Daily Value Saturated Fat:	15%

Nutrition Facts
Per Serving:

Calories	286
Total Fat	13 g
Saturated Fat	3 g
Cholesterol	70 mg
Sodium	427 mg
Carbohydrate	18 g
Fiber	5 g
Protein	26 g

Exchanges:
3 Lean Meat
3 Vegetable
1 Fat

Grilled Chicken With Black Bean Salsa

The combination of black beans, yellow corn, and red tomato makes a colorful topper. The salsa also can be served over grilled fish or flank steak, or as a snack with tortilla chips.

4	small skinless, boneless chicken breast halves (about 12 ounces total)
3	tablespoons lime juice
1	tablespoon honey
1	teaspoon paprika
½	teaspoon ground turmeric
⅛	teaspoon garlic powder
	Dash salt
	Dash ground red pepper

1	15-ounce can black beans, rinsed and drained
½	cup frozen whole kernel corn, cooked and drained
1	small tomato, chopped
2	tablespoons snipped fresh cilantro
1	jalapeño pepper, seeded and finely chopped*
	Tomato wedges (optional)

Rinse chicken; pat dry with paper towels. Combine 1 tablespoon of the lime juice, the honey, paprika, turmeric, garlic powder, salt, and red pepper. Brush over both sides of chicken breasts. Let stand 30 minutes. Grill chicken on the rack of an uncovered grill directly over medium coals for 12 to 15 minutes or until tender and no longer pink, turning once.

Meanwhile, in a medium bowl combine the beans, corn, chopped tomato, cilantro, jalapeño pepper, and the remaining 2 tablespoons lime juice. Serve with the chicken. If desired, garnish with tomato wedges. Makes 4 servings.

*Note: Because chili peppers, such as jalapeños, contain volatile oils that can burn your skin and eyes, avoid direct contact with them as much as possible. When working with chili peppers, wear plastic gloves. If your bare hands touch the chili peppers, wash your hands well with soap and water.

Total Fat: 3 g
Daily Value Fat: 5%
Saturated Fat: 1 g
Daily Value Saturated Fat: 5%

Nutrition Facts
Per Serving:

Calories	202
Total Fat	3 g
Saturated Fat	1 g
Cholesterol	45 mg
Sodium	340 mg
Carbohydrate	25 g
Fiber	5 g
Protein	24 g

Exchanges:
1½ Starch
2 Lean Meat
1 Vegetable

Prep time: 10 minutes **Standing time:** 30 minutes **Grilling time:** 12 minutes

Garlic-Clove Chicken

The garlic in this dish mellows in flavor as it bakes. For ease, you can leave the skins on the garlic cloves. To enjoy the buttery soft garlic, cut the skin and remove the clove with the tip of a knife.

1½ to 2 pounds meaty chicken pieces (breasts, thighs, and drumsticks), skinned
Nonstick spray coating
25 cloves garlic (about ½ cup or 2 to 3 bulbs)

¼ cup dry white wine
¼ cup reduced-sodium chicken broth
Salt
Ground red pepper

Rinse chicken; pat dry with paper towels. Spray an unheated large skillet with nonstick coating. Preheat over medium heat. Add chicken and cook for 10 minutes, turning to brown evenly.

Place chicken in a 2-quart square baking dish. Add unpeeled garlic cloves.

In a small bowl combine wine and chicken broth; pour over chicken. Lightly sprinkle chicken with salt and ground red pepper.

Bake, covered, in a 325° oven for 45 to 50 minutes or until chicken is tender and no longer pink. Makes 4 servings.

Total Fat:	6 g
Daily Value Fat:	9%
Saturated Fat:	2 g
Daily Value Saturated Fat:	10%

Nutrition Facts
Per Serving:

Calories	184
Total Fat	6 g
Saturated Fat	2 g
Cholesterol	69 mg
Sodium	140 mg
Carbohydrate	6 g
Fiber	0 g
Protein	23 g

Exchanges:
3 Lean Meat
1 Vegetable

Prep time: 15 minutes   **Baking time:** 45 minutes

Nutrition Facts

Hot 'n' Sweet Barbecued Chicken

Another time, pair this finger-licking sauce with grilled or broiled pork chops or sirloin steak.

¼ cup salsa
¼ cup catsup
¼ cup orange marmalade
1 tablespoon vinegar
½ teaspoon chili powder
½ teaspoon Worcestershire sauce
2 to 2½ pounds meaty chicken pieces (breasts, thighs, and drumsticks), skinned

For sauce, in a small bowl stir together salsa, catsup, marmalade, vinegar, chili powder, and Worcestershire sauce.

Rinse chicken; pat dry with paper towels. In a covered grill arrange medium-hot coals around a drip pan. Test for medium heat above the drip pan.* Place chicken on grill rack over drip pan, but not over coals. Lower the grill hood. Grill for 50 to 60 minutes or until tender and no longer pink. Brush chicken generously with sauce during the last 10 minutes of grilling. (Or, arrange the chicken in a 2-quart rectangular baking pan. Bake, uncovered, in a 375° oven for 30 minutes. Brush chicken generously with the sauce; bake for 10 to 15 minutes more or until tender and no longer pink.) Makes 4 servings.

*Note: To check for medium heat, hold your hand, palm side down, over where the meat will cook and at about the same height of the meat. The heat is right when you can hold your hand there for only 4 seconds.

Prep time: 10 minutes   **Grilling time:** 50 minutes

Paella

Paella (pi-AY-yuh) hails from Spain and boasts a saffron-spiced rice. Saffron, an integral ingredient in traditional paella, is costly, but a little goes a long way. Saffron is harvested from the purple crocus flower.

8 ounces fresh or frozen medium shrimp

1½ pounds meaty chicken pieces (breasts, thighs, and drumsticks)

Nonstick spray coating

1 cup chopped onion

1 clove garlic, minced

1 14½-ounce can reduced-sodium chicken broth

1 7½-ounce can tomatoes, undrained and cut up

1 teaspoon snipped fresh thyme or ¼ teaspoon dried thyme, crushed

¼ teaspoon ground saffron

⅛ to ¼ teaspoon ground red pepper

1 cup uncooked long grain rice

1 medium red or green sweet pepper, coarsely chopped

1 cup frozen peas

Thaw shrimp, if frozen. Peel and devein shrimp. Rinse shrimp and chicken; pat dry with paper towels. Cover and refrigerate until needed.

Spray an unheated Dutch oven with nonstick coating. Preheat over medium heat. Add onion and garlic. Cook until onion is tender.

Add chicken pieces, chicken broth, undrained tomatoes, thyme, saffron, and ground red pepper. Bring to boiling; reduce heat. Simmer, covered, for 15 minutes.

Stir in rice. Simmer, covered, about 15 minutes more or until rice is nearly tender. Stir shrimp, sweet pepper, and peas into the rice mixture. Simmer, covered, about 5 minutes more or until the rice and chicken are tender and shrimp turn pink. Makes 6 servings.

Prep time: 30 minutes **Cooking time:** 35 minutes

Nutrition Facts

Total Fat:	5 g
Daily Value Fat:	8%
Saturated Fat:	1 g
Daily Value Saturated Fat:	5%

Nutrition Facts
Per Serving:

Calories	274
Total Fat	5 g
Saturated Fat	1 g
Cholesterol	90 mg
Sodium	363 mg
Carbohydrate	33 g
Fiber	2 g
Protein	24 g

Exchanges:
1½ Starch
2 Lean Meat
2 Vegetable

Fiesta Chicken

Tomato sauces subtly sweetened with raisins are often found in Mexican cooking. This dish features tender chicken and raisins in a chili-spiced sauce that gets a boost of citrus flavor from orange juice.

Total Fat:	**3 g**
Daily Value Fat:	**5%**
Saturated Fat:	**1 g**
Daily Value Saturated Fat:	**5%**

Nutrition Facts
Per Serving:

Calories	255
Total Fat	3 g
Saturated Fat	1 g
Cholesterol	45 mg
Sodium	392 mg
Carbohydrate	37 g
Fiber	2 g
Protein	20 g

Exchanges:
1½ Starch
2 Lean Meat
1 Vegetable
½ Fruit

1	**8-ounce can tomato sauce**
½	**cup orange juice**
½	**cup finely chopped onion**
2	**tablespoons raisins**
2	**tablespoons chopped pimiento**
1½	**teaspoons snipped fresh oregano or ½ teaspoon dried oregano, crushed**
½	**teaspoon chili powder**
1	**clove garlic, minced**
	Several dashes bottled hot pepper sauce
12	**ounces skinless, boneless chicken breast halves**
1	**tablespoon cold water**
2	**teaspoons cornstarch**
2	**cups hot cooked rice**
¼	**cup snipped fresh parsley**

In a large skillet combine tomato sauce, orange juice, onion, raisins, pimiento, oregano, chili powder, garlic, and hot pepper sauce. Bring to boiling; reduce heat. Simmer, covered, for 5 minutes.

Meanwhile, rinse chicken; pat dry with paper towels. Cut into 2-inch pieces. Stir chicken pieces into skillet; return to boiling. Simmer, covered, for 12 to 15 minutes more or until chicken is tender and no longer pink.

Meanwhile, stir together cold water and cornstarch. Stir into mixture in skillet. Cook and stir until thickened and bubbly. Cook and stir for 2 minutes more.

Toss rice with parsley. Serve chicken mixture over rice. Makes 4 servings.

Start to finish: 40 minutes

Baked Chimichangas

Use leftover roasted chicken or turkey or roast beef or pork for this Mexican favorite. Freeze any extra chimichangas for another meal (see directions, below).

Total Fat:	**9 g**	
Daily Value Fat:	**14%**	
Saturated Fat:	**3 g**	
Daily Value Saturated Fat:	**15%**	

Nutrition Facts
Per Serving:

Calories	258
Total Fat	9 g
Saturated Fat	3 g
Cholesterol	37 mg
Sodium	685 mg
Carbohydrate	28 g
Fiber	3 g
Protein	18 g

Exchanges:
1½ Starch
2 Lean Meat
1 Vegetable

8 ounces cooked chicken, turkey, pork, or beef (1½ cups)
1 16-ounce can fat-free refried beans
1 8-ounce jar salsa
1 4½-ounce can diced green chili peppers, drained
3 tablespoons thinly sliced green onions

4 ounces reduced-fat Monterey Jack or cheddar cheese, shredded (1 cup)
8 8- to 9-inch flour tortillas
Salsa (optional)
Fat-free dairy sour cream (optional)
Thinly sliced green onion (optional)

Using 2 forks, shred cooked poultry, pork, or beef. In a large skillet combine poultry or meat, beans, the 1 jar salsa, the chili peppers, and the 3 tablespoons green onions. Cook and stir over medium heat until heated through. Stir in cheese.

Meanwhile, wrap tortillas in foil; warm in a 350° oven for 10 minutes. For each chimichanga, spoon about ½ cup of the meat mixture onto a tortilla, near one edge. Fold in sides; roll up.

Place in a 13×9×2-inch baking pan. Bake, uncovered, in a 350° oven for 15 to 20 minutes or until heated through and tortillas are crisp and brown. If desired, serve chimichangas with additional salsa, sour cream, and/or additional green onion. Makes 8 servings.

Freezing Directions: Place the unbaked chimichangas in freezer containers. Seal, label, and freeze for up to 6 months. To prepare, wrap the frozen chimichangas individually in foil. Bake in a 350° oven for 50 minutes. (Or, thaw chimichangas in refrigerator overnight. Wrap each in foil and bake about 30 minutes.) Remove the foil. Bake for 10 minutes more or until tortilla is crisp and brown.

Prep time: 25 minutes   **Baking time:** 15 minutes

Nutrition Facts

Grilled Chicken Salad

To streamline this hearty salad, begin the night before you plan to serve it. Start the chicken marinating and prepare the dressing (cover and refrigerate both). Opt for packaged torn salad greens to save even more time.

4   small skinless, boneless chicken breast halves (about 12 ounces total)
¼   cup frozen orange juice concentrate, thawed
2   teaspoons finely shredded lemon peel
2   tablespoons lemon juice
2   teaspoons olive oil
2   cloves garlic, minced
½   cup fat-free mayonnaise dressing or salad dressing
2   tablespoons milk
1   tablespoon frozen orange juice concentrate, thawed
1   tablespoon coarse-grain brown mustard
¼   teaspoon pepper
6   cups torn mixed greens
2   medium apples, cored and thinly sliced
1   tablespoon broken walnuts, toasted (optional)

Rinse chicken; pat dry with paper towels. Place in a plastic bag set in a shallow dish. For marinade, stir together the ¼ cup orange juice concentrate, the lemon peel, lemon juice, oil, and garlic. Pour over chicken. Close bag. Marinate in the refrigerator for 6 to 24 hours, turning bag occasionally.

For dressing, in a bowl stir together mayonnaise dressing, milk, the 1 tablespoon orange juice concentrate, the mustard, and pepper. Cover; chill until serving time.

Drain chicken, discarding marinade. Grill chicken on the rack of an uncovered grill directly over medium coals for 12 to 15 minutes or until chicken is tender and no longer pink, turning once. Arrange mixed greens and apple slices on 4 plates.

To serve, cut chicken breast halves into slices. Arrange slices on top of greens; drizzle with dressing. If desired, sprinkle with walnuts. Makes 4 servings.

Prep time: 30 minutes   **Marinating time:** 6 hours   **Grilling time:** 12 minutes

Nutrition Facts

Total Fat:	4 g
Daily Value Fat:	6%
Saturated Fat:	1 g
Daily Value Saturated Fat:	5%

Nutrition Facts
Per Serving:

Calories	202
Total Fat	4 g
Saturated Fat	1 g
Cholesterol	45 mg
Sodium	502 mg
Carbohydrate	23 g
Fiber	3 g
Protein	19 g

Exchanges:
2 Lean Meat
1 Vegetable
1 Fruit

Dilled Chicken And Potato Salad

No time to cook the chicken? Use chopped roasted chicken from the deli instead.

1 pound whole tiny new potatoes, quartered	1 cup chopped green pepper
12 ounces skinless, boneless chicken breast halves	½ cup nonfat Italian salad dressing
1 tablespoon olive oil or cooking oil	2 tablespoons snipped fresh dill
	1 tablespoon Dijon-style mustard
1 cup sliced celery	2 large tomatoes, halved and sliced
	1 medium cucumber, thinly sliced

Cook the potatoes, covered, in boiling salted water for 6 to 8 minutes or until tender; drain well.

Meanwhile, rinse chicken; pat dry with paper towels. Cut into bite-size strips. In a large skillet cook chicken in hot oil over medium-high heat for 3 to 4 minutes or until tender and no longer pink.

In a large bowl place cooked potatoes, cooked chicken, celery, and green pepper. Toss gently. In a small bowl stir together salad dressing, dill, and mustard. Drizzle over salad, tossing gently to coat.

Arrange sliced tomatoes and cucumber on 4 dinner plates. Spoon potato mixture over tomatoes and cucumber. If desired, garnish with additional fresh dill. Makes 4 servings.

Nutrition Facts

Total Fat:	**7 g**
Daily Value Fat:	**11%**
Saturated Fat:	**1 g**
Daily Value Saturated Fat:	**5%**

Nutrition Facts
Per Serving:

Calories	283
Total Fat	7 g
Saturated Fat	1 g
Cholesterol	45 mg
Sodium	597 mg
Carbohydrate	36 g
Fiber	4 g
Protein	20 g

Exchanges:
2 Starch
2 Meat
1 Vegetable

Prep time: 10 minutes   **Cooking time:** 9 minutes

Apricot-Stuffed Grilled Turkey Breast

Here's a tip from our Test Kitchen: Use kitchen shears to snip the dried apricots. It's easier, faster, and less messy than a knife and cutting board.

1	2- to 2½-pound bone-in turkey breast half	1	tablespoon cooking oil
1½	cups soft bread crumbs (2 slices)	¼	teaspoon dried rosemary, crushed
½	cup snipped dried apricots	¼	teaspoon garlic salt
¼	cup chopped pecans, toasted	1	tablespoon Dijon-style mustard
2	tablespoons apple juice or water	1	tablespoon water

Remove bone from turkey breast. Rinse turkey; pat dry with paper towels. Cut a horizontal slit into thickest part of turkey breast to form a 5×4-inch pocket. Set aside.

For stuffing, in a medium mixing bowl combine bread crumbs, apricots, pecans, apple juice or water, oil, rosemary, and garlic salt. Spoon stuffing into pocket. Securely fasten the opening with water-soaked wooden toothpicks or tie with heavy cotton string. Stir together mustard and water; set aside.

In a covered grill arrange medium-hot coals around a drip pan. Test for medium heat above the drip pan.* Place turkey on the grill rack over drip pan, but not over coals. Lower the grill hood. Grill about 1 hour or until turkey juices run clear (stuffing should reach 160°), brushing with mustard mixture during the last 15 minutes of cooking. Cover turkey with foil and let stand for 15 minutes before slicing. Makes 8 servings.

*Note: To check for medium heat, hold your hand, palm side down, over where the meat will cook and at about the same height of the meat. The heat is right when you can hold your hand there for only 4 seconds.

Nutrition Facts

Total Fat:	11 g
Daily Value Fat:	17%
Saturated Fat:	2 g
Daily Value Saturated Fat:	10%

Nutrition Facts
Per Serving:

Calories	237
Total Fat	11 g
Saturated Fat	2 g
Cholesterol	59 mg
Sodium	205 mg
Carbohydrate	10 g
Fiber	1 g
Protein	24 g

Exchanges:
½ Starch
3 Meat
½ Fruit

Prep time: 25 minutes   **Grilling time:** 1 hour   **Standing time:** 15 minutes

Turkey with Tomato Relish

The crumb coating on these turkey steaks is made from salsa-flavored crackers. Of course, you can try any type of reduced-fat crackers you like. An easy stir-together relish adds the finishing touch.

Nutrition Facts
Per Serving:

Calories	164
Total Fat	6 g
Saturated Fat	1 g
Cholesterol	37 mg
Sodium	490 mg
Carbohydrate	11 g
Fiber	1 g
Protein	18 g

Exchanges:
2 Lean Meat
2 Vegetable

4 turkey breast tenderloin steaks (about 12 ounces total)
   Nonstick spray coating
½ cup finely crushed reduced-fat salsa-flavored or reduced-fat cheese-flavored crackers
¼ teaspoon ground cumin
¼ teaspoon celery seed
1 tablespoon margarine or butter, melted

1 14½-ounce can diced tomatoes, drained
1 4½-ounce can diced green chili peppers, drained
½ cup finely chopped onion
2 to 4 tablespoons snipped fresh cilantro
1 tablespoon vinegar
1 teaspoon sugar
⅛ teaspoon salt

Rinse turkey; pat dry with paper towels. Spray a 2-quart rectangular baking dish with nonstick coating. Set aside.

In a shallow dish combine crushed crackers, cumin, and celery seed. Coat turkey with crushed cracker mixture. Place in the prepared dish. Drizzle with the melted margarine or butter. Bake, uncovered, in a 375° oven about 30 minutes or until turkey is tender and no longer pink.

Meanwhile, for relish, in a medium mixing bowl combine the drained tomatoes, chili peppers, onion, and cilantro. Stir in the vinegar, sugar, and salt. Cover and refrigerate until serving time. Serve turkey with the relish. If desired, garnish with additional fresh cilantro. Makes 4 servings.

Prep time: 20 minutes   **Baking time:** 30 minutes

Turkey-Mushroom Marsala

Shiitake mushrooms impart a rich earthy flavor to this delicate wine glaze. Discard the stems and use only the caps. Serve the turkey with linguine, if you like (a ¾-cup serving has about 105 calories or 1½ starches).

4 turkey breast tenderloin steaks (about 1 pound total)
1 cup sliced shiitake mushrooms
⅓ cup dry Marsala or dry sherry
⅓ cup water
1½ teaspoons snipped fresh thyme or ½ teaspoon dried thyme, crushed
1 teaspoon snipped fresh rosemary or ¼ teaspoon dried rosemary, crushed
⅛ teaspoon salt
⅛ teaspoon pepper
2 teaspoons olive oil or cooking oil
2 teaspoons cold water
1 teaspoon cornstarch
Hot cooked linguine (optional)

Rinse turkey; pat dry with paper towels. Place in a plastic bag set in a shallow dish.

For marinade, combine the mushrooms, Marsala or sherry, the ⅓ cup water, the thyme, rosemary, salt, and pepper. Pour over turkey. Close bag. Marinate in refrigerator for at least 30 minutes or up to 2 hours, turning bag occasionally.

Remove turkey from marinade, reserving marinade; pat dry. In a large skillet heat oil over medium heat. Cook turkey in hot oil for 8 to 10 minutes or until tender and no longer pink, turning once. Remove turkey; cover and keep warm. Add marinade to skillet. Bring to boiling; reduce heat. Simmer, covered, for 2 minutes.

Stir together the 2 teaspoons cold water and the cornstarch; stir into mixture in skillet. Cook and stir until thickened and bubbly. Cook and stir for 2 minutes more. If desired, serve turkey and mushroom mixture over linguine and garnish with additional fresh rosemary. Makes 4 servings.

Prep time: 25 minutes   **Marinating time:** 30 minutes   **Cooking time:** 15 minutes

Orange-Sesame Turkey Kabobs

Kabobs are a perfect plan-ahead meal. Cut up your vegetables ahead of time, place them in a sealable plastic bag, and store them in the refrigerator. When it's time to cook, all you have left to do is skewer and grill.

12 ounces turkey breast tenderloin steaks
¼ cup frozen orange juice concentrate, thawed
2 teaspoons sesame seed
1½ teaspoons snipped fresh thyme or ½ teaspoon dried thyme, crushed
1 teaspoon toasted sesame oil
¼ teaspoon salt

2 cups desired fresh vegetables (such as 1-inch pieces red and/or green sweet pepper, whole mushrooms, 1-inch-thick half-slices zucchini or yellow summer squash, and whole cherry tomatoes)
Nonstick spray coating
Hot cooked linguine (optional)
Orange wedges (optional)

Rinse turkey; pat dry with paper towels. Cut into 1-inch pieces.

For marinade, in a shallow dish combine orange juice concentrate, sesame seed, thyme, sesame oil, and salt. Add turkey, stirring to coat. Cover; marinate at room temperature for 30 minutes or in the refrigerator for up to 2 hours. Drain, reserving marinade.

Alternately thread turkey and vegetables onto long skewers. (If using tomatoes, add to end of skewers for the last 1 minute of grilling.) Brush with remaining marinade.

Spray an unheated grill rack with nonstick coating. Grill kabobs on prepared rack of an uncovered grill directly over medium coals for 12 to 14 minutes or until turkey is tender and no longer pink, turning occasionally to cook evenly. If desired, serve over linguine and garnish with orange wedges. Makes 4 servings.

Nutrition Facts

Total Fat:	**4 g**
Daily Value Fat:	**6%**
Saturated Fat:	**1 g**
Daily Value Saturated Fat:	**5%**

Nutrition Facts
Per Serving:

Calories	146
Total Fat	4 g
Saturated Fat	1 g
Cholesterol	37 mg
Sodium	171 mg
Carbohydrate	10 g
Fiber	1 g
Protein	18 g

Exchanges:
2 Lean Meat
1 Vegetable
½ Fruit

Prep time: 20 minutes   **Marinating time:** 30 minutes   **Grilling time:** 12 minutes

Ginger Turkey Meat Loaf

To make sure you're buying lean ground turkey, read the label to be certain that it does not contain any skin. Otherwise, ask your butcher to grind turkey breast for you without added skin.

Nutrition Facts
Per Serving:

Calories	200
Total Fat	10 g
Saturated Fat	3 g
Cholesterol	78 mg
Sodium	289 mg
Carbohydrate	10 g
Fiber	0 g
Protein	18 g

Exchanges:
3 Lean Meat
½ Fruit

Nonstick spray coating
1 beaten egg
1 beaten egg white
1 cup soft whole wheat bread crumbs (about 1⅓ slices)
½ cup finely chopped green onions
1 2-ounce jar diced pimiento, drained
2 tablespoons reduced-sodium soy sauce
1 tablespoon milk or water
¼ teaspoon pepper
1½ pounds ground raw turkey
2 tablespoons apricot preserves
¼ teaspoon ground ginger
Fresh tomato wedges (optional)
Fresh sage (optional)

Spray a 9×5×3-inch loaf pan with nonstick coating. Set aside.

In a large bowl combine the egg, egg white, bread crumbs, green onions, pimiento, soy sauce, milk or water, and pepper. Add the ground turkey; mix well. Press mixture into the prepared pan, patting to smooth the top. Bake, uncovered, in a 350° oven for 45 minutes.

Meanwhile, in a small bowl stir together the apricot preserves and ginger; brush over surface of loaf. Bake 10 to 15 minutes more or until no longer pink. Remove from oven; pour off any drippings. Let stand for 5 minutes; invert onto a plate. Turn right side up for slicing. If desired, garnish with tomato wedges and fresh sage. Makes 6 servings.

Prep time: 20 minutes   **Baking time:** 55 minutes   **Standing time:** 5 minutes

Nutrition Facts

Basil Turkey Burgers

What a treat this burger is from regular burgers. The dried tomato mayonnaise adds a special touch to the basil-infused burgers. If possible, use fresh basil leaves for the best flavor.

¼ cup fat-free milk

2 tablespoons finely chopped onion

1 tablespoon fine dry bread crumbs

1 tablespoon snipped fresh basil or 1 teaspoon dried basil, crushed

⅛ teaspoon salt

⅛ teaspoon pepper

12 ounces ground raw turkey

4 lettuce leaves

4 hamburger buns, split and toasted

¼ cup Dried Tomato Mayonnaise

In a medium mixing bowl combine the milk, onion, bread crumbs, basil, salt, and pepper. Add ground turkey; mix well. Shape mixture into four ¾-inch-thick patties.

Grill patties on the rack of an uncovered grill directly over medium coals for 14 to 18 minutes or until no longer pink, turning once. (Or, place patties on the unheated rack of a broiler pan. Broil 4 inches from the heat for 12 to 14 minutes or until no longer pink, turning once.)

To serve, place a lettuce leaf on the bottom half of each bun and top with 1 of the patties. Spoon 1 tablespoon of the Dried Tomato Mayonnaise on top of each patty. Place bun tops on top of the burgers. Makes 4 servings.

Dried Tomato Mayonnaise: In a small mixing bowl pour enough boiling water over 2 tablespoons snipped dried tomatoes (not oil-pack) to cover. Let stand about 10 minutes or until tomatoes are pliable. Drain well. Stir tomatoes into ⅓ cup fat-free mayonnaise dressing or light mayonnaise dressing. Cover and store leftovers in the refrigerator. Makes about ½ cup.

Prep time: 20 minutes   **Grilling time:** 14 minutes

Cassoulet

The calories and fat of this simplified version of the classic French dish have been pared down substantially from traditional cassoulet. To reduce the sodium, replace the canned beans with cooked dried beans (see note, below).

Nutrition Facts

Total Fat:	5 g
Daily Value Fat:	8%
Saturated Fat:	1 g
Daily Value Saturated Fat:	5%

Nutrition Facts
Per Serving:

Calories	315
Total Fat	5 g
Saturated Fat	1 g
Cholesterol	25 mg
Sodium	1,266 mg
Carbohydrate	47 g
Fiber	3 g
Protein	23 g

Exchanges:
2½ Starch
2 Lean Meat
2 Vegetable

Nonstick spray coating
4 ounces smoked turkey sausage, cut into bite-size pieces
4 ounces lean boneless pork, cubed
1 cup chopped onion
1 cup chopped carrot
1 cup sliced celery
2 cloves garlic, minced

1 14½-ounce can reduced-sodium chicken broth
1 8-ounce can low-sodium tomato sauce
½ teaspoon dried thyme, crushed
1 bay leaf
2 15-ounce cans navy beans, rinsed and drained

Spray an unheated large saucepan with nonstick coating. Preheat over medium heat. Add the turkey sausage, pork, onion, carrot, celery, and garlic. Cook and stir until pork is brown on all sides and vegetables are nearly tender.

Stir in the chicken broth, tomato sauce, thyme, and bay leaf. Bring to boiling; reduce heat. Simmer, covered, about 1 hour or until pork is tender, stirring occasionally.

Stir in beans. Simmer, uncovered, for 20 to 30 minutes more or until of desired consistency. Discard bay leaf. Makes 5 servings.

Note: To cook dried beans, rinse 8 ounces of navy beans. In a large Dutch oven combine the beans and 4 cups cold water. Bring to boiling; reduce heat. Simmer for 2 minutes. Remove from heat. Cover and let stand for 1 hour. Drain and rinse. In same pan combine beans and 4 cups fresh water. Bring to boiling; reduce heat. Simmer, covered, for 1 to 1½ hours or until beans are tender.

Prep time: 20 minutes   Cooking time: 1 hour and 20 minutes

Fish
& Seafood

Grilled Tuna with Tuscan Beans
See Recipe, Page 48

The catch of the day
are these **succulent entrées**
that artfully combine
fresh fish and seafood with
bold-flavored ingredients.

Crunchy-Topped Fish with Potatoes

This oven-fried version of fish and chips makes for great family dining. Stuffing mix contributes the crunchy coating for the fish.

Total Fat:	**14 g**
Daily Value Fat:	**22%**
Saturated Fat:	**3 g**
Daily Value Saturated Fat:	**15%**

Nutrition Facts
Per Serving:

Calories	317
Total Fat	14 g
Saturated Fat	3 g
Cholesterol	63 mg
Sodium	358 mg
Carbohydrate	26 g
Fiber	1 g
Protein	22 g

Exchanges:
1½ Starch
3 Lean Meat
½ Fat

4 **4-ounce fresh or frozen catfish or other fish fillets, ½ to ¾ inch thick**
   Nonstick spray coating
2 **medium baking potatoes (12 ounces total), cut into 3×½×½-inch sticks**

2 **teaspoons cooking oil**
   Garlic salt or seasoned pepper
¾ **cup herb-seasoned stuffing mix, crushed**
1 **tablespoon margarine or butter, melted**
1 **tablespoon water**

Thaw fish, if frozen. Rinse fish; pat dry with paper towels. Set aside.

Line a large shallow baking pan with foil. Spray the foil with nonstick coating. Arrange potato sticks in a single layer over half of the baking sheet. Brush the potatoes with the oil. Sprinkle with the garlic salt or seasoned pepper. Bake in a 450° oven for 10 minutes.

Meanwhile, stir together the stuffing mix, the melted margarine or butter, and the water. Place fish on baking sheet next to potatoes, tucking under any thin edges of the fish for an even thickness. Sprinkle stuffing mixture over fish. Return pan to oven and bake for 9 to 12 minutes more or until fish flakes easily when tested with a fork and potatoes are tender. Makes 4 servings.

Prep time: 15 minutes   **Baking time:** 19 minutes

Spicy Broiled Shark Steaks

To check for doneness of fish, stick the tines of a fork into the thickest portion of the fish at a 45-degree angle. Then gently twist the fork and pull up some of the flesh. If the fish flakes easily, it's done.

1 pound fresh or frozen shark or swordfish steaks, cut ¾ inch thick
2 green onions, thinly sliced
2 tablespoons orange juice
2 tablespoons chili sauce
1 tablespoon snipped fresh basil or 1 teaspoon dried basil, crushed

1 tablespoon finely chopped fresh ginger
1 tablespoon reduced-sodium soy sauce
Several dashes hot chili oil
Nonstick spray coating
Orange slices (optional)
Fresh chives (optional)

Thaw fish, if frozen. Rinse fish; pat dry with paper towels. Cut into 4 serving-size portions. For marinade, in a shallow bowl combine the green onions, orange juice, chili sauce, basil, ginger, soy sauce, and chili oil. Add the fish, turning to coat with marinade. Cover; marinate at room temperature for 20 minutes.

Spray the unheated rack of a broiler pan with nonstick coating. Drain fish, reserving marinade. Place fish on prepared rack. Broil 4 inches from the heat for 5 minutes. Using a wide spatula, carefully turn fish over. Brush with the reserved marinade. Broil for 5 to 7 minutes more or until fish flakes easily when tested with a fork. If desired, serve fish on top of orange slices and garnish with fresh chives. Makes 4 servings.

Nutrition Facts

Total Fat:	**5 g**
Daily Value Fat:	**8%**
Saturated Fat:	**1 g**
Daily Value Saturated Fat:	**5%**

Nutrition Facts
Per Serving:

Calories	160
Total Fat	5 g
Saturated Fat	1 g
Cholesterol	45 mg
Sodium	342 mg
Carbohydrate	3 g
Fiber	0 g
Protein	23 g

Exchanges:
3 Lean Meat

Prep time: 15 minutes   **Marinating time:** 20 minutes   **Broiling time:** 10 minutes

Grilled Tuna With Tuscan Beans

Tuna and beans—tonno e fagioli—is a favorite combination in Italian coastal towns. Using canned beans makes our version fast and easy. (Also pictured on pages 44–45.)

Total Fat:	**7 g**
Daily Value Fat:	**10%**
Saturated Fat:	**1 g**
Daily Value Saturated Fat:	**5%**

Nutrition Facts
Per Serving:

Calories	298
Total Fat	7 g
Saturated Fat	1 g
Cholesterol	49 mg
Sodium	536 mg
Carbohydrate	25 g
Fiber	5 g
Protein	33 g

Exchanges:
1½ Starch
3 Very Lean Meat
1 Vegetable
½ Fat

1 pound fresh or frozen tuna, swordfish, halibut, shark, or salmon steaks	2 teaspoons snipped fresh sage or ¼ teaspoon ground sage
2 cloves garlic, minced	1 15-ounce can small white beans, rinsed and drained
1 tablespoon olive oil	2 teaspoons olive oil
1 14½-ounce can Italian-style stewed tomatoes, undrained and cut up	2 teaspoons lemon juice
	⅛ teaspoon pepper
	Nonstick spray coating

Thaw fish, if frozen. For beans, in a medium skillet cook the garlic in 1 tablespoon hot oil for 15 seconds. Stir in the undrained tomatoes and the sage. Bring to boiling; reduce heat. Simmer, uncovered, for 5 minutes. Stir in beans; heat through.

Meanwhile, rinse fish; pat dry with paper towels. Measure thickness of fish. Cut fish into 4 serving-size portions. Brush both sides of fish with the 2 teaspoons oil and the lemon juice; sprinkle with pepper.

Spray an unheated grill rack or grill basket with nonstick coating. Place fish on prepared rack or in prepared grill basket. Grill on an uncovered grill directly over medium-hot coals until fish flakes easily when tested with a fork (allow 4 to 6 minutes per ½-inch thickness of fish). If the fish is more than 1 inch thick, gently turn it halfway through grilling. (Or, place fish on the greased unheated rack of a broiler pan. Broil 4 inches from the heat for 4 to 6 minutes per ½-inch thickness. If the fish is more than 1 inch thick, gently turn it halfway through broiling.)

To serve, remove the skin from fish. Spoon beans on each serving plate and top with fish. If desired, garnish with additional fresh sage. Makes 4 servings.

Prep time: 15 minutes   **Grilling time:** Depends on thickness of fish

Parmesan Baked Fish

Quick, easy, slimming, and delicious—what more can you ask of a recipe? Keep the meal simple by adding a vegetable, and for dessert, indulge in your favorite flavor of fat-free ice cream.

4 4-ounce fresh or frozen skinless salmon or other firm fish fillets, ¾ to 1 inch thick
Nonstick spray coating
¼ cup light mayonnaise dressing or salad dressing

2 tablespoons grated Parmesan cheese
1 tablespoon snipped fresh chives or sliced green onion
1 teaspoon white wine Worcestershire sauce

Thaw fish, if frozen. Rinse fish; pat dry with paper towels. Spray a 2-quart square or rectangular baking dish with nonstick coating. Set aside.

In a small bowl stir together mayonnaise dressing or salad dressing, Parmesan cheese, chives or green onion, and Worcestershire sauce. Spread the mayonnaise mixture over fish fillets; place in the baking dish.

Bake, uncovered, in a 450° oven for 12 to 15 minutes or until fish flakes easily when tested with a fork. If desired, garnish with additional fresh chives. Makes 4 servings.

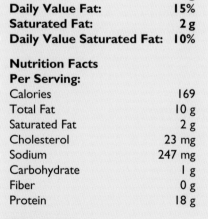

Total Fat:	10 g
Daily Value Fat:	15%
Saturated Fat:	2 g
Daily Value Saturated Fat:	10%

Nutrition Facts
Per Serving:

Calories	169
Total Fat	10 g
Saturated Fat	2 g
Cholesterol	23 mg
Sodium	247 mg
Carbohydrate	1 g
Fiber	0 g
Protein	18 g

Exchanges:
3 Lean Meat

Prep time: 15 minutes   **Baking time:** 12 minutes

Italian Fish Soup

In Italy, there are as many versions of zuppa di pesce, or fish soup, as there are coastal towns. Serve fish soup as the Italians do—topped with a slice of toasted Italian bread.

Total Fat: 3 g
Daily Value Fat: 4%
Saturated Fat: 0 g
Daily Value Saturated Fat: 0%

Nutrition Facts
Per Serving:
Calories 252
Total Fat 3 g
Saturated Fat 0 g
Cholesterol 96 mg
Sodium 780 mg
Carbohydrate 30 g
Fiber 5 g
Protein 24 g

Exchanges:
1½ Starch
2 Very Lean Meat
2 Vegetable

8 ounces fresh or frozen haddock, bass, sole, or other fish fillets

6 ounces fresh or frozen peeled and deveined shrimp

3 cups water

2 medium tomatoes, peeled and cut up

1 cup thinly sliced carrots (2 medium)

½ cup chopped celery

½ cup dry white wine or water

⅓ cup chopped onion

2 teaspoons instant chicken bouillon granules

½ teaspoon dried marjoram, crushed

½ teaspoon finely shredded orange peel

2 cloves garlic, minced

2 bay leaves
    Dash bottled hot pepper sauce

¼ cup tomato paste

4 slices Italian bread, toasted

Thaw the fish fillets and shrimp, if frozen. Rinse fish and shrimp; pat dry with paper towels. Cut the fish into 1-inch pieces; halve shrimp lengthwise. Chill.

In a large saucepan combine the 3 cups water, the tomatoes, carrots, celery, wine or water, onion, bouillon granules, marjoram, orange peel, garlic, bay leaves, and hot pepper sauce. Bring to boiling; reduce heat. Cover and simmer for 15 to 20 minutes or until vegetables are nearly tender. Stir in tomato paste.

Add fish pieces and shrimp to saucepan. Bring mixture just to boiling; reduce heat. Cover and simmer about 5 minutes more or until fish flakes easily when tested with a fork and shrimp turn pink. Discard bay leaves.

To serve, ladle into soup bowls. Place a slice of Italian bread on each serving. Serve immediately. Makes 4 servings.

Prep time: 20 minutes   **Cooking time:** 20 minutes

Nutrition Facts

Chilled Cod With Gazpacho Sauce

All you need are five ingredients for this lazy-day summertime salad. Choose from both eat-now or eat-later chilling options.

Total Fat:	**5 g**
Daily Value Fat:	**8%**
Saturated Fat:	**1 g**
Daily Value Saturated Fat:	**5%**

Nutrition Facts
Per Serving:

Calories	136
Total Fat	5 g
Saturated Fat	1 g
Cholesterol	43 mg
Sodium	234 mg
Carbohydrate	4 g
Fiber	1 g
Protein	19 g

Exchanges:
2 Lean Meat
1 Vegetable

8 ounces fresh or frozen cod, cusk, flounder, or orange roughy fillets, ½ inch thick
1 lemon, halved and sliced
¼ cup deli marinated cucumber salad or mixed vegetable salad, drained
¼ cup chunky salsa
2 cups torn mixed greens

Thaw fish, if frozen. Rinse fish; pat dry with paper towels. In a large skillet or saucepan place a large open steamer basket over ½ inch of water. Bring water to boiling; reduce heat. Carefully place the fish fillets in the steamer basket. (If necessary, cut the fish into 2 pieces to fit.) Top with half of the lemon slices. Cover and steam fish about 6 minutes or until fish flakes easily when tested with a fork. Discard lemon slices.

Remove fish from steamer basket. Carefully immerse the fish in a bowl of ice water. Let the fish stand in the ice water about 5 minutes or until thoroughly chilled. Remove fish from water; drain on paper towels. (Or, cover and refrigerate for 2 to 4 hours or until chilled.)

Meanwhile, for sauce, cut up any large pieces of cucumber or mixed vegetable salad. Stir together the salad and the salsa.

Arrange mixed greens on 2 dinner plates. Place the chilled fish on top of the greens. Spoon salsa mixture over fish. Garnish with remaining lemon slices. Makes 2 servings.

Start to finish: 25 minutes

Shrimp Creole

Shrimp are sold by the pound in a variety of sizes. Generally, the larger shrimp cost more with fewer per pound. Although we used large shrimp in this classic Louisiana dish, medium work fine, too.

12 ounces fresh or frozen peeled and deveined large shrimp
¾ cup chopped onion
¾ cup chopped green pepper
½ cup chopped celery
1 14½-ounce can Cajun-style or Mexican-style stewed tomatoes, undrained and cut up
2 tablespoons snipped fresh thyme or 1 teaspoon dried thyme, crushed

1 teaspoon instant chicken bouillon granules
1 teaspoon sugar
2 cloves garlic, minced
 Several dashes bottled hot pepper sauce (optional)
2 teaspoons cornstarch
2 cups hot cooked rice
¼ cup snipped fresh parsley or celery tops

Rinse shrimp. In a large saucepan bring 4 cups water to boiling; add shrimp. Return to boiling; reduce heat. Simmer, uncovered, for 1 to 3 minutes or until shrimp turn pink. Drain in colander. Set aside.

In same saucepan combine the onion, green pepper, celery, and ⅓ cup water. Bring to boiling; reduce heat. Simmer, covered, for 3 to 4 minutes or until vegetables are crisp-tender. Do not drain.

Stir in undrained tomatoes, thyme, bouillon granules, sugar, garlic, and hot pepper sauce (if using). Simmer, covered, for 8 minutes.

Combine cornstarch and 1 tablespoon cold water; stir into saucepan. Cook and stir over medium heat until thickened and bubbly; reduce heat. Cook and stir for 2 minutes more. Stir in shrimp; heat through. Combine rice and parsley or celery tops. Serve shrimp mixture with rice. Makes 4 servings.

Start to finish: 45 minutes

Nutrition Facts

Szechwan Shrimp

Szechwan peppers generally supply the heat in Szechwan cooking. In this recipe, convenient-to-use crushed red pepper steps in. If you like milder foods, reduce the red pepper to $1/4$ or even $1/8$ teaspoon.

1 pound fresh or frozen shrimp in shells
3 tablespoons water
2 tablespoons catsup
1 tablespoon reduced-sodium soy sauce
1 tablespoon rice wine, dry sherry, or water
2 teaspoons cornstarch
1 teaspoon honey
1 teaspoon grated fresh ginger or $1/4$ teaspoon ground ginger
$1/2$ teaspoon crushed red pepper
1 tablespoon peanut oil or cooking oil
$1/2$ cup sliced green onions
4 cloves garlic, minced
2 cups hot cooked rice

Thaw shrimp, if frozen. Peel and devein shrimp; cut in half lengthwise. Rinse; pat dry with paper towels. Set aside.

For sauce, in a small mixing bowl stir together the 3 tablespoons water; the catsup; soy sauce; rice wine, sherry, or water; cornstarch; honey; ground ginger (if using); and crushed red pepper. Set aside.

Pour oil into a large skillet or wok. Heat over medium-high heat. Add green onions, garlic, and grated fresh ginger (if using); stir-fry for 30 seconds.

Add shrimp. Stir-fry for 2 to 3 minutes or until shrimp turn pink; push to side of skillet or wok. Stir sauce; add to center of skillet. Cook and stir until thickened and bubbly. Cook and stir for 2 minutes more. Serve with rice. Makes 4 servings.

Start to finish: 30 minutes

Nutrition Facts

Cheesy Crab And Broccoli

Sharp cheddar cheese boosts the flavor of the rich-tasting sauce. Here we've used regular—not lower-fat—cheese. Lower-fat cheese may not work as well here. Prolonged or high-temperature cooking causes it to toughen.

2 cups frozen cut broccoli

6 ounces refrigerated crab-flavored fish pieces or one 6-ounce can crabmeat, drained, flaked, and cartilage removed

1 tablespoon margarine or butter

2 cups sliced fresh mushrooms

1 clove garlic, minced

2 tablespoons all-purpose flour

⅛ teaspoon pepper

1 cup fat-free milk

¼ cup shredded sharp cheddar cheese (1 ounce)

2 tablespoons grated Parmesan cheese

2 tablespoons crushed rich round crackers (about 3 crackers)

Cook the broccoli according to package directions; drain. In 4 individual 14- to 16-ounce au gratin dishes or oval casseroles arrange broccoli and crab-flavored fish pieces or canned crabmeat. Set dishes aside.

For sauce, in medium saucepan melt the margarine or butter over medium-high heat. Add mushrooms and garlic and cook about 4 minutes or until mushrooms are tender. Stir in flour and pepper. Add milk all at once. Cook and stir until thickened and bubbly; remove from heat. Stir in cheddar cheese until melted.

Spoon sauce over broccoli and fish in dishes. Cover dishes with foil. Bake in a 400° oven for 8 to 10 minutes or until bubbly. (If desired, refrigerate unbaked casseroles for 2 to 24 hours. To serve, bake, covered, in a 400° oven for 20 to 25 minutes or until bubbly.) Combine Parmesan cheese and crushed crackers; sprinkle over casseroles. Makes 4 servings.

Nutrition Facts

Total Fat:	8 g
Daily Value Fat:	12%
Saturated Fat:	3 g
Daily Value Saturated Fat:	15%

Nutrition Facts
Per Serving:

Calories	188
Total Fat	8 g
Saturated Fat	3 g
Cholesterol	19 mg
Sodium	565 mg
Carbohydrate	17 g
Fiber	3 g
Protein	14 g

Exchanges:
1 Lean Meat
2 Vegetable
½ Milk
½ Fat

Prep time: 25 minutes   **Baking time:** 8 minutes

Crab and Fennel Risotto

Fennel is a celerylike vegetable that has a delicate licorice flavor. The seed from the fennel plant is a spice traditionally used in Italian sausage.

2 fennel bulbs with tops
1 cup sliced fresh mushrooms, such as shiitake, porcini, or button
½ teaspoon fennel seed, crushed
1 tablespoon olive oil
1 cup uncooked Arborio or medium grain rice
3¼ cups water
1 teaspoon instant chicken bouillon granules
⅛ teaspoon pepper
1 cup cooked crabmeat; one 6-ounce can crabmeat, drained, flaked, and cartilage removed; or one 6-ounce package frozen crabmeat, thawed and drained
½ cup asparagus,* cut into 1-inch pieces
⅓ cup thinly sliced green onions

Trim fennel bulbs, reserving tops. Quarter bulbs lengthwise and slice. Measure 1 cup sliced fennel. Snip enough of the fennel tops to get 1 tablespoon; set aside. In a large saucepan cook the 1 cup fennel, the mushrooms, and fennel seed in hot oil until tender. Stir in rice. Cook and stir over medium heat for 2 minutes.

Carefully stir in water, bouillon granules, and pepper. Bring to boiling; reduce heat. Cover and simmer for 20 minutes (do not lift cover).

Remove saucepan from heat. Stir in crabmeat, asparagus, and green onions. Let stand, covered, for 5 minutes. (The rice should be tender but slightly firm, and the mixture should be creamy. If necessary, stir in a little water to reach the desired consistency.)

Stir in the snipped fennel tops. If desired, garnish with additional fennel tops. Makes 4 servings.

*Note: If using thick asparagus spears, halve spears lengthwise, cut into 1-inch pieces, and cook in a small amount of boiling water until crisp-tender. Add to risotto.

Prep time: 20 minutes   **Cooking time:** 20 minutes

Nutrition Facts

Total Fat:	5 g
Daily Value Fat:	7%
Saturated Fat:	1 g
Daily Value Saturated Fat:	5%

**Nutrition Facts
Per Serving:**

Calories	307
Total Fat	5 g
Saturated Fat	1 g
Cholesterol	22 mg
Sodium	401 mg
Carbohydrate	54 g
Fiber	6 g
Protein	13 g

Exchanges:
2½ Starch
½ Lean Meat
2½ Vegetable
½ Fat

Clam-Corn Chowder

If you plan to tote the soup for lunch, make it the night before. Cover and refrigerate it. In the morning, heat the soup on the stove. Carry it in a preheated insulated vacuum bottle (see below).

½ cup chopped celery
¼ cup chopped onion
1 tablespoon margarine or butter
¼ cup all-purpose flour
1½ teaspoons snipped fresh marjoram or ½ teaspoon dried marjoram, crushed
1½ teaspoons snipped fresh thyme or ½ teaspoon dried thyme, crushed
½ teaspoon dry mustard
¼ teaspoon pepper
2⅔ cups fat-free milk
1 8-ounce bottle clam juice
1 teaspoon instant chicken bouillon granules
1 15-ounce can cream-style corn
1 6½-ounce can minced clams, drained

In a large saucepan cook celery and onion in hot margarine or butter until tender. Stir in flour, marjoram, thyme, mustard, and pepper. Add the milk, clam juice, and bouillon granules all at once.

Cook and stir until thickened and bubbly. Cook and stir for 1 minute more. Stir in corn and clams; heat through. (If desired, divide chowder among 4 airtight containers. Store up to 3 days in the refrigerator.) If desired, garnish with additional fresh herb. Makes 4 servings.

To tote for lunch: If using chilled soup, transfer to a small saucepan. Heat soup just to boiling, stirring often. Transfer hot soup to a preheated insulated vacuum bottle. (To preheat the bottle, fill with hot tap water. Cover with lid; let stand about 5 minutes. Pour out water and immediately fill with the hot soup.)

Start to finish: 30 minutes

Nutrition Facts	
Total Fat:	5 g
Daily Value Fat:	8%
Saturated Fat:	1 g
Daily Value Saturated Fat:	5%

Nutrition Facts
Per Serving:

Calories	257
Total Fat	5 g
Saturated Fat	1 g
Cholesterol	34 mg
Sodium	796 mg
Carbohydrate	35 g
Fiber	2 g
Protein	21 g

Exchanges:

1 Starch
1 Lean Meat
1 Vegetable
1 Milk

Shrimp and Fruit Salad

Treat yourself to a spectacular luncheon salad. The flavorful lemon-mint dressing perfectly complements the shrimp, pineapple, and orange combination.

12 ounces fresh or frozen peeled
    and deveined shrimp
 1 15¼-ounce can pineapple
    chunks (juice-packed)
 1 medium orange, peeled and
    sectioned
 1 tablespoon snipped fresh mint
    or 1 teaspoon dried mint,
    crushed

   Dash salt
   Dash pepper
½ cup sliced celery
½ cup lemon low-fat yogurt
 4 cantaloupe wedges (optional)

In a large saucepan cook shrimp in a large amount of boiling water for 1 to 3 minutes or until shrimp turn pink. Drain. Rinse under cold water; drain well.

Drain pineapple chunks, reserving ¼ cup juice. Combine pineapple chunks and orange sections; cover and refrigerate.

For marinade, in a medium bowl combine the reserved pineapple juice, the mint, salt, and pepper. Stir in cooked shrimp and the celery. Cover and marinate in the refrigerator for 2 hours. Drain, discarding marinade.

Stir the pineapple mixture into shrimp mixture. Fold in the yogurt. If desired, serve over cantaloupe wedges. Store leftovers, covered, in the refrigerator for up to 2 days. Makes 4 servings.

To tote for lunch: Place 1 serving in an airtight container. If desired, place a cantaloupe wedge in a self-sealing plastic bag. Carry the salad and cantaloupe wedge in an insulated lunch box with a frozen ice pack. To serve, spoon the salad over the cantaloupe wedge.

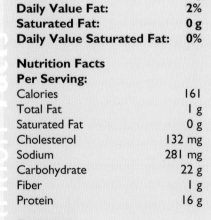

Total Fat:	1 g
Daily Value Fat:	2%
Saturated Fat:	0 g
Daily Value Saturated Fat:	0%

Nutrition Facts
Per Serving:
Calories	161
Total Fat	1 g
Saturated Fat	0 g
Cholesterol	132 mg
Sodium	281 mg
Carbohydrate	22 g
Fiber	1 g
Protein	16 g

Exchanges:
2 Lean Meat
1½ Fruit

Prep time: 25 minutes   **Marinating time:** 2 hours

Pasta Dinners

Chicken and Penne
With Basil Sauce
See Recipe, Page 62

Smoothly switching roles
from salads to soups
to international specialties,
ever-popular pasta
speeds the way to good eating
in these no-fuss meal makers.

Hot Oriental Beef and Pasta

Hoisin sauce, a condiment made of soybeans, garlic, chili peppers, and various spices, is also called Peking sauce.

12 ounces boneless beef top sirloin steak, cut 1 inch thick
4 ounces packaged dried spaghetti or vermicelli, broken, or corkscrew macaroni
¼ cup orange juice
2 tablespoons hoisin sauce
1 tablespoon reduced-sodium soy sauce
½ teaspoon toasted sesame oil
⅛ teaspoon ground red pepper
Nonstick spray coating
1 clove garlic, minced
10 ounces fresh asparagus, cut into 1-inch pieces (about 2 cups)
1 medium carrot, cut into thin strips
1 small red onion, cut into wedges

Trim fat from beef. Partially freeze beef. Thinly slice across the grain into bite-size strips. Set aside.

Cook pasta according to package directions, except omit any oil and salt. Drain pasta. Cover and keep warm.

Meanwhile, for sauce, stir together orange juice, hoisin sauce, soy sauce, sesame oil, and red pepper. Set aside.

Spray an unheated wok or 12-inch skillet with nonstick coating. Preheat over medium-high heat. Add garlic; stir-fry for 15 seconds. Add asparagus and carrot; stir-fry for 1 minute. Add onion; stir-fry for 2 to 3 minutes more or until vegetables are crisp-tender. Remove vegetables from wok or skillet.

Add beef to wok or skillet. Stir-fry about 3 minutes or until desired doneness. Return vegetables to wok or skillet. Drizzle sauce over all. Toss to coat all ingredients. Heat through. Serve over pasta. Makes 4 servings.

Prep time: 30 minutes   **Cooking time:** 10 minutes

Nutrition Facts

Total Fat:	9 g
Daily Value Fat:	14%
Saturated Fat:	3 g
Daily Value Saturated Fat:	16%

Nutrition Facts
Per Serving:

Calories	331
Total Fat	9 g
Saturated Fat	3 g
Cholesterol	57 mg
Sodium	353 mg
Carbohydrate	35 g
Fiber	2 g
Protein	26 g

Exchanges:
2 Starch
2½ Lean Meat
1 Vegetable

Bolognese Meat Sauce with Pasta

Traditionally, Bolognese (boh-luh-NEEZ) sauce is full of meat. We've cut back on fat and calories by substituting lentils for part of the meat.

2 tablespoons finely chopped pancetta or bacon (optional)
12 ounces extra-lean ground beef
2 14½-ounce cans low-sodium tomatoes, undrained and cut up
1 cup chopped onion
¾ cup dry lentils
¼ cup finely chopped carrot
¼ cup finely chopped celery
¼ cup snipped fresh parsley
⅓ of a 6-ounce can tomato paste (¼ cup)
1 teaspoon instant beef bouillon granules
1 cup water
½ cup dry white wine or beef broth
12 ounces packaged dried pasta, such as penne, spaghetti, or cavatelli
⅓ cup evaporated fat-free milk
Grated Parmesan cheese (optional)
Celery leaves (optional)

In a large saucepan or kettle cook pancetta or bacon (if using) just until crisp. Add ground beef; cook until meat is no longer pink. Drain well.

If desired, pass undrained tomatoes through a food mill or sieve. Or, process in blender or food processor until nearly smooth. For sauce, add the tomatoes, onion, lentils, carrot, celery, parsley, tomato paste, and bouillon granules to meat. Stir in the water and wine or broth. Bring to boiling; reduce heat. Cover and simmer about 40 minutes or until lentils are tender, stirring occasionally. Uncover and simmer about 5 minutes more or until of desired consistency.

Meanwhile, cook pasta according to package directions. Drain well.

Stir evaporated milk into meat mixture; heat through. Serve sauce over pasta. If desired, top with Parmesan cheese and garnish with celery leaves. Makes 6 servings.

Prep time: 15 minutes   **Cooking time:** 45 minutes

Nutrition Facts

Chicken and Penne with Basil Sauce

If fresh basil is unavailable, do not substitute dried basil. Use another fresh herb instead, such as thyme, sage, or tarragon. Dried herbs just can't compare to the flavor of fresh herbs used here. (Also pictured on pages 58–59.)

1¼ cups reduced-sodium chicken broth

4 teaspoons cornstarch

⅛ teaspoon black pepper

2 cups packaged dried penne or corkscrew macaroni

12 ounces skinless, boneless chicken breast halves
Nonstick spray coating

1 medium red sweet pepper, cut into thin strips

1 medium yellow or green sweet pepper, cut into thin strips

3 cloves garlic, minced

1 tablespoon cooking oil

¼ cup lightly packed fresh basil leaves, cut into thin shreds

2 tablespoons finely shredded Parmesan cheese

Stir together chicken broth, cornstarch, and black pepper. Set aside.

Cook pasta according to package directions, omitting any oil and salt. Drain. Cover; keep warm.

Meanwhile, rinse chicken; pat dry with paper towels. Cut into 1-inch cubes; set aside. Spray an unheated large skillet with nonstick coating. Preheat over medium heat. Add sweet peppers and garlic. Stir-fry for 2 to 3 minutes or until sweet peppers are crisp-tender. Remove from skillet. Add the oil to skillet; increase heat to medium high. Add the chicken; stir-fry for 3 to 4 minutes or until chicken is no longer pink.

Stir broth mixture; add to skillet. Cook and stir until thickened and bubbly. Return sweet peppers to skillet; add the basil shreds. Cook and stir for 2 minutes more. Toss with hot pasta. Sprinkle with Parmesan cheese. If desired, garnish with additional fresh basil. Makes 4 servings.

Start to finish: 25 minutes

Total Fat:	8 g
Daily Value Fat:	12%
Saturated Fat:	1 g
Daily Value Saturated Fat:	5%

Nutrition Facts
Per Serving:

Calories	330
Total Fat	8 g
Saturated Fat	1 g
Cholesterol	47 mg
Sodium	282 mg
Carbohydrate	39 g
Fiber	1 g
Protein	24 g

Exchanges:
2 Starch
2 Lean Meat
2 Vegetable

Chicken, Long Beans, & Tomato Stir-Fry

If you think good taste is hard to measure, consider Chinese long beans. A star of Asian stir-fries, these dark green, pencil-thin legumes average 1½ feet of meaty, crunchy flavor. Many supermarkets now stock them. (Also pictured on the cover.)

12 ounces skinless, boneless chicken breast halves
1 teaspoon Cajun seasoning or other spicy seasoning blend
6 ounces wide rice noodles or packaged dried egg noodles
4 teaspoons cooking oil
2 cloves garlic, minced

1 pound Chinese long beans or whole green beans, cut into 3-inch pieces
¼ cup water
2 medium tomatoes, cut into thin wedges
2 tablespoons raspberry vinegar

Rinse chicken; pat dry with paper towels. Cut into strips. Toss chicken with Cajun seasoning; set aside.

Cook rice noodles in boiling, lightly salted water for 3 to 5 minutes or until tender. Or, cook egg noodles according to package directions. Drain noodles; keep warm.

Meanwhile, in a large skillet heat 2 teaspoons of the oil. Add garlic and stir-fry for 15 seconds. Add beans; stir-fry for 2 minutes. Carefully add water to skillet. Reduce heat to low; cover and simmer for 6 to 8 minutes or until beans are crisp-tender. Remove beans from skillet.

Add the remaining 2 teaspoons cooking oil to skillet. Add chicken; stir-fry for 3 to 4 minutes or until no longer pink. Add beans, tomatoes, and vinegar; heat through. Serve over noodles. Makes 4 servings.

Start to finish: 30 minutes

Spicy Pasta Pie

Vermicelli is thinner than thin spaghetti but thicker than angel hair pasta. In this dish, it creates the crust to hold a spicy sausage sauce.

4 ounces packaged dried vermicelli, broken
1 beaten egg white
  Nonstick spray coating
1 cup shredded mozzarella cheese (4 ounces)
1 pound turkey breakfast sausage
1 cup sliced fresh mushrooms
½ cup chopped onion
1 clove garlic, minced

1 7½-ounce can low-sodium tomatoes, undrained and cut up
½ of a 6-ounce can (⅓ cup) tomato paste
1 teaspoon dried Italian seasoning, crushed
⅛ teaspoon crushed red pepper
2 tablespoons grated Parmesan or Romano cheese
  Celery leaves (optional)

Cook vermicelli according to package directions, except omit any oil and salt. Drain well. Toss with the egg white. Spray a 9-inch quiche dish or pie plate with nonstick coating. Press vermicelli mixture into bottom of prepared dish. Sprinkle with mozzarella cheese. Set aside.

Meanwhile, in a large skillet cook the turkey sausage, mushrooms, onion, and garlic until sausage is no longer pink and onion is tender. Drain off fat. Stir in the undrained tomatoes, tomato paste, Italian seasoning, and crushed red pepper. Pour sausage mixture over cheese layer.

Cover dish loosely with foil. Bake in a 350° oven for 25 to 30 minutes or until heated through. Sprinkle with the Parmesan or Romano cheese. Let stand 10 minutes. If desired, garnish with the celery leaves. Cut pie into wedges to serve. Makes 6 servings.

Nutrition Facts

Total Fat:	**14 g**
Daily Value Fat:	**22%**
Saturated Fat:	**6 g**
Daily Value Saturated Fat:	**30%**

Nutrition Facts
Per Serving:

Calories	316
Total Fat	14 g
Saturated Fat	6 g
Cholesterol	41 mg
Sodium	732 mg
Carbohydrate	22 g
Fiber	1 g
Protein	26 g

Exchanges:
1 Starch
3 Medium-Fat Meat
1 Vegetable

Prep time: 25 minutes   **Baking time:** 25 minutes   **Standing time:** 10 minutes

Tuna-Pasta Salad

This dressed-up macaroni salad features carrot and red sweet pepper, in addition to tuna. Simply add some crusty rolls for a complete meal.

3 ounces packaged dried corkscrew macaroni (about 1 cup)
1 medium carrot, thinly sliced
½ of a medium cucumber, quartered lengthwise and sliced
½ of a red sweet pepper, chopped
2 green onions, sliced
⅓ cup reduced-calorie creamy Italian or ranch salad dressing
1 6-ounce can low-sodium chunk light tuna, drained
Romaine or lettuce leaves or thinly sliced tomato

Cook pasta according to package directions, except omit any oil and salt. Drain. Rinse with cold water; drain.

In a large mixing bowl toss together drained pasta, carrot, cucumber, sweet pepper, and onions. Add salad dressing. Toss until well mixed. Gently stir in tuna. Cover and refrigerate for 2 to 6 hours.

Arrange the greens or tomato on 4 plates. Spoon the tuna mixture on top of the greens or tomato. Makes 4 servings.

Nutrition Facts

Total Fat:	**3 g**
Daily Value Fat:	**5%**
Saturated Fat:	**0 g**
Daily Value Saturated Fat:	**0%**

Nutrition Facts
Per Serving:

Calories	166
Total Fat	3 g
Saturated Fat	0 g
Cholesterol	1 mg
Sodium	261 mg
Carbohydrate	22 g
Fiber	2 g
Protein	13 g

Exchanges:
1 Starch
1 Lean Meat
1 Vegetable

Prep time: 25 minutes   **Chilling time:** 2 hours

Jalapeño Shrimp and Pasta

Rely on a touch of fresh jalapeños when you want to add spunk to a dish. To keep fresh peppers on hand for easy use, slice or chop them, then freeze them for up to 6 months.

Nutrition Facts

Total Fat:	**5 g**
Daily Value Fat:	**8%**
Saturated Fat:	**1 g**
Daily Value Saturated Fat:	**5%**

Nutrition Facts
Per Serving:

Calories	345
Total Fat	5 g
Saturated Fat	1 g
Cholesterol	131 mg
Sodium	338 mg
Carbohydrate	51 g
Fiber	2 g
Protein	23 g

Exchanges:
3 Starch
1½ Meat
1 Vegetable

12 ounces fresh or frozen shrimp
1 tablespoon margarine or butter
1 medium onion, chopped
1 fresh jalapeño pepper, seeded and chopped*
¼ teaspoon ground cumin
¼ teaspoon black pepper
⅛ teaspoon salt
2 cloves garlic, minced

2 medium tomatoes, chopped (1⅓ cups)
1 4½-ounce can diced green chili peppers, drained
8 ounces packaged dried penne, rigatoni, or cavatelli, cooked and drained
Fresh chili peppers (optional)

Thaw shrimp, if frozen. Peel and devein shrimp; halve any large shrimp. Rinse and pat dry with paper towels. In a 10-inch skillet heat margarine or butter over medium-high heat. Add shrimp, onion, jalapeño pepper, cumin, black pepper, salt, and garlic. Cook, stirring frequently, for 1 to 3 minutes or until shrimp turn pink.

Gently stir in tomatoes and green chili peppers. Heat through. Serve immediately over hot cooked pasta. If desired, garnish with chili peppers. Makes 4 servings.

*Note: Because chili peppers, such as jalapeños, contain volatile oils that can burn your skin and eyes, avoid direct contact with them as much as possible. When working with chili peppers, wear plastic gloves. If your bare hands touch the chili peppers, wash your hands well with soap and water.

Prep time: 15 minutes   **Cooking time:** 8 minutes

Fettuccine with Garlic Scallops

Dried tomatoes that are not packed in oil need to be rehydrated in boiling water. Their intensity lends a wonderful flavor punch to this elegant dish.

1 pound fresh or frozen scallops
6 dried tomato halves (not oil-packed)
⅓ cup boiling water
2 teaspoons cooking oil
3 large cloves garlic, minced
2 cups sliced fresh mushrooms
2 tablespoons lemon juice
2 teaspoons cornstarch

4 green onions, sliced
2 tablespoons snipped fresh parsley
½ teaspoon finely shredded lemon peel
3 cups hot cooked spinach and/or plain fettuccine
Lemon wedges (optional)

Thaw scallops, if frozen. Rinse and pat dry with paper towels. In a small bowl combine dried tomatoes and boiling water. Let stand 10 minutes. Drain tomatoes, reserving liquid. Cut tomatoes into thin bite-size strips. Set aside.

Pour oil into a large nonstick skillet. Heat over medium-high heat. Add garlic and stir-fry for 15 seconds. Add mushrooms; stir-fry for 2 minutes. Add scallops and tomatoes; stir-fry for 2 to 3 minutes or until scallops are opaque.

Combine lemon juice and cornstarch. Add to skillet along with reserved tomato liquid, green onions, parsley, and lemon peel. Cook and stir until slightly thickened and bubbly. Cook and stir for 2 minutes more.

Serve the scallop mixture over hot pasta. If desired, garnish with lemon wedges. Makes 4 servings.

Start to finish: 35 minutes

Pasta alla Carbonara with Asparagus

Traditionally, a raw egg is used in this sauce. By substituting a pasteurized egg product, you can be sure your dish will be safe for you and your family. If you can't find pecorino cheese, which is made from sheep's milk, Parmesan cheese is a suitable substitute.

2   cups 1-inch pieces asparagus
    or one 10-ounce package
    frozen cut asparagus
3   slices turkey bacon or bacon,
    sliced crosswise into thin strips
1   clove garlic, minced
1   cup evaporated fat-free milk
¼   cup refrigerated or frozen egg
    product, thawed

8   ounces packaged dried fusilli,
    spaghetti, or fettuccine
2   teaspoons margarine or butter
½   cup freshly grated pecorino or
    Parmesan cheese
¼   cup snipped fresh parsley
    Freshly ground black pepper

In a small saucepan cook fresh asparagus in a small amount of boiling water for 4 to 6 minutes or until crisp-tender. (Or, cook the frozen asparagus according to package directions.) Drain and set aside.

In a small nonstick skillet cook bacon and garlic until bacon is crisp. Drain on paper towels. Set aside. In a medium bowl stir together the milk and egg product. Set aside.

Cook pasta according to package directions, except omit any oil and salt. Drain well. Return to hot kettle. Immediately pour the egg mixture over the pasta. Add the margarine or butter. Heat and stir mixture over medium-low heat for 5 to 6 minutes or until mixture thickens and pasta is well coated. Add the asparagus, cooked bacon mixture, cheese, and parsley; toss until combined. To serve, transfer pasta to a large serving dish. Sprinkle with black pepper. Makes 4 servings.

Prep time: 22 minutes   **Cooking time:** 5 minutes

Lo Mein With Tofu

Look for soba noodles, a type of Japanese pasta made from buckwheat flour, at Asian specialty markets or in the oriental food section of your supermarket.

2	cups broccoli flowerets
1	cup thinly sliced carrots
4	ounces extra-firm light tofu (fresh bean curd), cut into ½-inch cubes
1	cup cold water
2	tablespoons reduced-sodium soy sauce
4	teaspoons cornstarch
½	teaspoon instant vegetable bouillon granules

8	ounces soba noodles (buckwheat noodles) or packaged dried spaghetti
	Nonstick spray coating
1	teaspoon toasted sesame oil
1	cup sliced fresh mushrooms
4	large green onions, cut into ½-inch pieces
2	teaspoons grated fresh ginger
2	cloves garlic, minced
1	tablespoon olive oil
2	teaspoons toasted sesame seed

In a covered medium saucepan cook broccoli and carrots in a small amount of boiling water for 3 to 4 minutes or until crisp-tender; drain. Pat the tofu dry with paper towels. Stir together the cold water, soy sauce, cornstarch, and bouillon granules; set aside. Cook noodles or spaghetti according to package directions until tender but still firm, except omit any oil and salt. Drain and keep warm.

Spray an unheated nonstick wok or large skillet with nonstick coating. Add ½ teaspoon of the sesame oil; heat over medium-high heat. Add mushrooms, green onions, ginger, and garlic. Stir-fry for 1 to 2 minutes or until crisp-tender. Remove. Add olive oil and remaining sesame oil to wok. Add tofu; stir-fry for 1 to 2 minutes or just until tofu starts to brown. Remove. Add broccoli mixture and mushroom mixture to wok; push from center. Stir soy sauce mixture; add to center of wok. Cook and stir until thickened and bubbly. Add noodles. Using 2 spatulas or forks, lightly toss for 3 to 4 minutes or until noodles are heated through. Add tofu; toss lightly. Cover; cook 1 to 2 minutes or until heated through. To serve, sprinkle with sesame seed. Makes 4 servings.

Start to finish: 25 minutes

Nutrition Facts

Total Fat:	5 g
Daily Value Fat:	8%
Saturated Fat:	1 g
Daily Value Saturated Fat:	5%

Nutrition Facts
Per Serving:

Calories	241
Total Fat	5 g
Saturated Fat	1 g
Cholesterol	0 mg
Sodium	704 mg
Carbohydrate	43 g
Fiber	3 g
Protein	10 g

Exchanges:
2 Starch
2 Vegetable
1 Fat

Meatless
Main Dishes

Curried Vegetable
Stir-Fry
See Recipe, Page 75

If you feel a meal without meat doesn't pass muster, try these **stick-to-the-ribs** recipes and discover the **health benefits** and **taste delights** of beans, whole grains, and legumes.

Vegetable Lasagna with Red Pepper Sauce

In a hurry? Substitute 2 cups of prepared spaghetti sauce for the Red Pepper Sauce in this recipe.

6 no-boil lasagna noodles or packaged dried regular lasagna noodles

8 ounces zucchini and/or yellow summer squash, halved and sliced

2 cups sliced fresh mushrooms

⅓ cup chopped onion

2 teaspoons olive oil

1 cup fat-free ricotta cheese

¼ cup finely shredded Parmesan cheese

Red Pepper Sauce

1 cup shredded part-skim mozzarella cheese

1 medium tomato, seeded and chopped

Fresh oregano (optional)

Soak the no-boil lasagna noodles in warm water for 10 minutes. (Or, cook regular noodles according to package directions, except omit salt.) Meanwhile, in large skillet cook and stir squash, mushrooms, and onion in hot oil about 6 minutes or until tender. Drain well. Combine ricotta, Parmesan, and ¼ teaspoon black pepper. To assemble, place 3 lasagna noodles in a 2-quart square baking dish, trimming to fit as necessary. Top with ricotta mixture, half of the vegetable mixture, half of the Red Pepper Sauce, and half of the mozzarella. Layer with remaining noodles, vegetables, and sauce.

Bake, uncovered, in a 375° oven for 30 minutes. Sprinkle with remaining mozzarella cheese and the tomato; bake 5 minutes more or until heated through. Let stand 10 minutes before serving. If desired, garnish with fresh oregano. Makes 6 servings.

Red Pepper Sauce: In a large skillet cook 3 cups chopped red sweet peppers and 4 whole cloves garlic in 1 tablespoon olive oil over medium heat about 20 minutes, stirring occasionally. (Or, use one 12-ounce jar roasted red sweet peppers, drained. Omit cooking step.) Transfer to a blender container. Cover; blend until nearly smooth. Add ½ cup water, ¼ cup tomato paste, 2 tablespoons red wine vinegar, and 1 tablespoon snipped fresh oregano. Cover; blend with several on-off turns until oregano is just chopped. Return to skillet; heat through. Makes about 2 cups.

Prep time: 55 minutes   **Baking time:** 35 minutes   **Standing time:** 10 minutes

Barley-Stuffed Cabbage Rolls

A blend of fennel, wild rice, walnuts, and barley fills these rolls. Fennel imparts a light licorice flavor. If you like, save the feathery leaves and use as a garnish.

⅓ cup uncooked wild rice	8 large cabbage leaves
1 cup vegetable broth or chicken broth	2 8-ounce cans low-sodium tomato sauce
½ cup pearl barley	1 tablespoon brown sugar
1 small fennel bulb, chopped (about ¾ cup)	Few dashes bottled hot pepper sauce
½ cup shredded carrot	Grated Parmesan cheese (optional)
1 tablespoon snipped fresh thyme or ½ teaspoon dried thyme, crushed	Fresh thyme or fennel leaves (optional)
¼ cup chopped walnuts, toasted	

Rinse wild rice in cold water; drain. In a saucepan heat 1¾ cups water and broth to boiling. Add rice and barley. Reduce heat; simmer, covered, for 30 minutes. Stir in fennel, carrot, and the 1 tablespoon or ½ teaspoon thyme. Simmer, covered, for 10 to 15 minutes or until rice and barley are tender. Drain; stir in walnuts.

Meanwhile, fill a large Dutch oven with water. Bring to boiling. Cut out center veins from cabbage leaves, keeping each leaf in 1 piece. Immerse leaves, 4 at a time, into the boiling water for 2 to 3 minutes or until leaves are limp. Drain well.

Place about ½ cup of the rice mixture on each cabbage leaf; fold in sides. Starting at an unfolded edge, carefully roll up each leaf. For sauce, stir together the tomato sauce, brown sugar, and hot pepper sauce. Spoon about ¾ cup of the sauce into a 2-quart square baking dish. Place cabbage rolls in dish. Spoon remaining sauce over cabbage rolls. Bake, covered, in a 400° oven about 25 minutes or until heated through. If desired, sprinkle with Parmesan cheese and garnish with additional fresh thyme or fennel leaves. Makes 4 servings.

Prep time: 55 minutes   **Baking time:** 25 minutes

Nutrition Facts

Total Fat:	**6 g**
Daily Value Fat:	**9%**
Saturated Fat:	**1 g**
Daily Value Saturated Fat:	**5%**

Nutrition Facts
Per Serving:

Calories	261
Total Fat	6 g
Saturated Fat	1 g
Cholesterol	0 mg
Sodium	302 mg
Carbohydrate	47 g
Fiber	9 g
Protein	9 g

Exchanges:
2 Starch
3 Vegetable
½ Fat

Greek Spinach Triangles

Using nonstick spray coating rather than butter between the sheets of phyllo dough gives a more healthful spin to this traditional Greek dish.

Total Fat:	**11 g**
Daily Value Fat:	**17%**
Saturated Fat:	**5 g**
Daily Value Saturated Fat:	**25%**

Nutrition Facts
Per Serving:

Calories	224
Total Fat	11 g
Saturated Fat	5 g
Cholesterol	132 mg
Sodium	540 mg
Carbohydrate	20 g
Fiber	0 g
Protein	13 g

Exchanges:
1 Starch
2 Medium-Fat Meat
1 Vegetable

⅔ cup chopped onion
2 tablespoons snipped fresh parsley
½ teaspoon dried oregano, crushed
¼ teaspoon ground nutmeg
¼ teaspoon pepper
2 egg whites
2 eggs
¼ cup fat-free milk
1 10-ounce package frozen chopped spinach, thawed and well drained
1 cup crumbled feta cheese (4 ounces)
   Nonstick spray coating
5 sheets frozen phyllo dough (18×14-inch rectangle), thawed
¼ cup fat-free dairy sour cream (optional)
⅛ teaspoon lemon-pepper seasoning (optional)

For filling, cook onion in a small amount of boiling water about 10 minutes or until very tender. Drain. Combine cooked onion, parsley, oregano, nutmeg, and pepper. In a medium bowl combine the egg whites, whole eggs, and milk. Beat with a rotary beater or a wire whisk until smooth. Stir in onion mixture, spinach, and feta cheese.

Spray the bottom of a 2-quart square baking dish with nonstick coating. Unfold phyllo sheets; cut into quarters (about 9×7 inches). (To prevent drying, keep phyllo sheets covered with plastic wrap until ready to use.) Place 1 quarter-sheet of phyllo in bottom of dish, folding as necessary to fit. Spray with nonstick coating. Repeat with 9 more quarter-sheets of phyllo and spray coating. Spread spinach mixture over phyllo in dish. Layer remaining quarter-sheets of phyllo over filling, spraying each with nonstick coating. Using a sharp knife, score top of phyllo dough into 8 triangles.

Bake, uncovered, in a 375° oven about 30 minutes or until golden. Let stand for 10 minutes. To serve, cut into triangles along scored lines. If desired, combine sour cream and lemon-pepper seasoning; spoon over phyllo triangles. Makes 4 servings.

Prep time: 25 minutes   **Baking time:** 30 minutes   **Standing time:** 10 minutes

Curried Vegetable Stir-Fry

This flavorful vegetable entrée fuses Asian stir-frying with curry and European Brussels sprouts. (Also pictured on pages 70–71.)

2 cups water
1¼ cups quick-cooking pearl barley
1 cup fresh Brussels sprouts or frozen Brussels sprouts, thawed
1 cup cold water
4 teaspoons cornstarch
1 to 2 teaspoons curry powder
1 teaspoon instant vegetable bouillon granules

Nonstick spray coating
1½ cups red, yellow, and/or green sweet pepper strips
2 tablespoons thinly sliced green onion
1 cup bias-sliced carrots
¼ cup peanuts

In a medium saucepan bring the 2 cups water to boiling. Slowly add the barley. Return to boiling; reduce heat. Simmer, covered, for 10 to 12 minutes or until barley is tender. If necessary, drain thoroughly.

Meanwhile, cut Brussels sprouts in half. In a saucepan cook Brussels sprouts in a small amount of boiling water for 3 minutes. Drain well. For sauce, stir together the 1 cup water, the cornstarch, curry powder, and bouillon granules. Set aside.

Spray an unheated wok or large skillet with nonstick coating. Preheat over medium-high heat. Add sweet peppers and green onion. Stir-fry for 1 minute. Stir in the Brussels sprouts and carrots. Stir-fry for 3 minutes more. Push the vegetables from center of wok. Stir sauce; add to the center of wok. Cook and stir until thickened and bubbly. Stir to coat all ingredients with sauce. Cook and stir for 2 minutes.* Serve immediately over barley. Sprinkle with peanuts. Makes 4 servings.

*Note: If desired, add 4 ounces extra-firm light tofu (fresh bean curd), cut into ½-inch cubes. Cover and cook about 30 seconds or until heated through.

Start to finish: 30 minutes

Triple Mushroom And Rice Fajitas

This earthy three-mushroom filling makes a satisfying meatless meal. Substitute button mushrooms if you can't find all three varieties of mushrooms in your supermarket.

½ cup uncooked regular brown rice
¼ cup water
2 tablespoons lime juice
1 tablespoon olive oil or cooking oil
2 large cloves garlic, minced
½ teaspoon ground cumin
½ teaspoon dried oregano, crushed
¼ teaspoon salt
3 ounces fresh portobello mushrooms, stemmed and thinly sliced

3 ounces fresh chanterelle or oyster mushrooms, thinly sliced
3 ounces fresh shiitake mushrooms, stemmed and thinly sliced
1 cup green and/or red sweet pepper strips
4 green onions, cut into 1½-inch pieces
8 7- to 8-inch flour tortillas
¼ cup slivered almonds, toasted
    Green onion tops (optional)
    Fresh cilantro (optional)

Cook brown rice according to package directions, except omit any salt.

Meanwhile, for marinade, in a large plastic bag set in a deep bowl combine the water, lime juice, olive or cooking oil, garlic, cumin, oregano, and salt. Add the mushrooms, pepper strips, and green onions. Close the bag; turn bag to coat vegetables. Marinate at room temperature for 15 to 30 minutes.

Wrap tortillas in foil. Heat in a 350° oven for 10 minutes to soften. For filling, in a nonstick large skillet cook *undrained* mushroom mixture over medium-high heat for 6 to 8 minutes or until peppers are tender and all but about 2 tablespoons of the liquid has evaporated, stirring occasionally. Stir in rice and almonds; heat through.

To serve, spoon mushroom-rice mixture onto tortillas; roll up. If desired, tie a green onion top around each tortilla and garnish with cilantro. Makes 4 servings.

Start to finish: 1 hour

Nutrition Facts

Grilled Vegetables On Focaccia

When grilled, vegetables take on a pleasant smoky flavor. Lay the vegetables perpendicular to the wires on the grill rack so the vegetables don't fall into the coals.

3 tablespoons balsamic vinegar or wine vinegar
2 tablespoons water
1 tablespoon olive oil
1 teaspoon dried oregano, crushed
2 large red and/or orange sweet peppers
2 medium zucchini and/or yellow summer squash, halved crosswise and sliced thinly lengthwise
1 medium eggplant, cut crosswise into ½-inch slices
2 ounces soft goat cheese (chèvre)
2 ounces fat-free cream cheese
1 purchased focaccia (about a 12-inch round)
Fresh oregano (optional)

In a small bowl combine vinegar, water, oil, and dried oregano. Set aside. Cut sweet peppers in quarters. Remove stems, membranes, and seeds. Arrange all vegetables on grill rack; brush with vinegar mixture. Grill on an uncovered grill directly over medium-hot coals until slightly charred, turning occasionally (allow 8 to 10 minutes for peppers and eggplant, and 5 to 6 minutes for squash). Cut peppers into strips.

In a small bowl combine the goat cheese and cream cheese. Set aside. Cut focaccia in half crosswise. Split halves into 2 layers horizontally to form 4 pieces total.

Spread goat cheese mixture over bottom layers of focaccia. Top with some of the sweet peppers, squash, and eggplant; place top halves of focaccia over vegetables. To serve, cut into wedges. If desired, garnish with fresh oregano. Makes 8 servings.

Prep time: 20 minutes   **Grilling time:** 8 minutes

Hoppin' John With Grits Polenta

According to tradition, eating hoppin' John on New Year's Day brings good luck. This appealing version has an Italian slant.

Grits Polenta
  Nonstick spray coating
¾ cup uncooked long grain rice
½ of a 16-ounce package frozen black-eyed peas or one 15-ounce can black-eyed peas, rinsed and drained
1½ cups chopped red, yellow, and/or green sweet peppers
1 cup thinly bias-sliced carrots
1 cup frozen whole kernel corn
1 tablespoon chopped shallots
4 cloves garlic, minced
2 teaspoons snipped fresh thyme
¼ teaspoon crushed red pepper
2 teaspoons olive oil or cooking oil
2 medium tomatoes, seeded and chopped
2 tablespoons snipped fresh parsley

Prepare Grits Polenta. Spray a 9-inch pie plate with nonstick coating. Spread the grits mixture into pan. Cover and chill overnight. Cook rice according to package directions, except omit any salt. If using frozen black-eyed peas, cook according to package directions; drain. Cook sweet peppers, carrots, corn, shallots, garlic, thyme, crushed red pepper, ¼ teaspoon salt, and ⅛ teaspoon black pepper in hot oil, covered, for 6 to 8 minutes or until crisp-tender. Stir in rice, peas, and tomatoes. Cook, covered, over low heat about 5 minutes or until hot, stirring occasionally. Stir in parsley.

Meanwhile, spray unheated rack of a broiler pan with nonstick coating. Cut polenta into 12 wedges; arrange on prepared rack. Broil 4 to 5 inches from heat for 4 to 5 minutes or until surface is slightly crisp and beginning to brown. Serve rice mixture with polenta. If desired, garnish with additional fresh thyme. Makes 6 servings.

Grits Polenta: In a medium saucepan combine 1⅓ cups water, ⅔ cup fat-free milk, and ⅛ teaspoon salt. Bring to boiling; reduce heat. Add ½ cup quick-cooking white (hominy) grits, stirring with a whisk. Cook and stir for 5 to 7 minutes or until very thick. Remove from heat. Stir in ½ cup shredded reduced-fat mozzarella cheese until melted.

Nutrition Facts

Total Fat:	**4 g**
Daily Value Fat:	**6%**
Saturated Fat:	**1 g**
Daily Value Saturated Fat:	**5%**

Nutrition Facts
Per Serving:

Calories	295
Total Fat	4 g
Saturated Fat	1 g
Cholesterol	6 mg
Sodium	244 mg
Carbohydrate	54 g
Fiber	5 g
Protein	12 g

Exchanges:
3 Starch
2 Vegetable

Prep time: 45 minutes   **Chilling time:** Overnight   **Cooking time:** 11 minutes

Tofu Pitas with Mango Salsa

Although the ingredients for Jamaican jerk seasoning differ from brand to brand, this Caribbean flavoring blend typically includes chili peppers, thyme, garlic, and onion. Look for it in the seasoning aisle of your supermarket.

Mango Salsa
2 tablespoons lime juice or lemon juice
1 teaspoon cooking oil
½ teaspoon Jamaican jerk seasoning
1 10½-ounce package firm light tofu (fresh bean curd)

Nonstick spray coating
⅓ cup couscous
3 large pita bread rounds, halved crosswise
Fresh spinach leaves or torn lettuce leaves

Prepare Mango Salsa. Cover and chill. Meanwhile, in a shallow dish combine the lime or lemon juice, oil, and Jamaican jerk seasoning. Slice tofu into ½-inch-thick slices. Lay slices in marinade and brush marinade over tofu slices. Marinate at room temperature for 30 minutes, turning slices once and brushing marinade over all, or marinate in the refrigerator for up to 6 hours.

Spray a grill basket with nonstick coating. Place tofu in prepared grill basket. Discard marinade. Grill tofu in basket on the rack of an uncovered grill directly over medium-hot coals about 10 minutes or until heated through. Cut tofu into cubes. (Or, spray an unheated broiler pan with nonstick coating. Lay tofu slices on the broiler pan. Broil 5 to 6 inches from the heat about 8 minutes or until heated through, turning once.)

Meanwhile, cook couscous according to package directions, except omit any butter and salt. Fluff with fork. To serve, add tofu and couscous to salsa; toss gently. Line pita halves with spinach or lettuce leaves. Spoon salsa mixture into pita halves. Makes 6 servings.

Mango Salsa: Combine 1 cup peeled and chopped mango; 1 small tomato, seeded and chopped; ½ of a medium cucumber, seeded and chopped; 1 thinly sliced green onion; 2 tablespoons snipped fresh cilantro; 1 fresh jalapeño pepper, seeded and chopped (see note, page 26); and 1 tablespoon lime or lemon juice. Makes 2 cups.

Prep time: 35 minutes **Marinating time:** 30 minutes **Grilling time:** 10 minutes

Double Corn Tortilla Casserole

Delve into this Southwestern-style strata and you'll find layers of corn tortillas, mozzarella cheese, and vegetables all baked in a savory custard.

Nonstick spray coating
1½ cups frozen whole kernel corn
6 6-inch corn tortillas
1 cup shredded reduced-fat mozzarella cheese (4 ounces)
½ cup sliced green onions
1 4-ounce can diced green chili peppers, drained
¼ cup finely chopped red sweet pepper
1 cup buttermilk
2 egg whites*
1 egg*
¼ teaspoon garlic salt
Fresh Italian parsley (optional)
⅓ cup salsa

Spray a 2-quart square baking dish with nonstick coating. In a medium saucepan cook corn according to package directions; drain well. Tear tortillas into bite-size pieces. Arrange half of the tortillas in baking dish. Top with half of the cheese, half of the corn, half of the green onions, half of the chili peppers, and half of the red sweet pepper. Repeat the layers using the remaining tortillas, cheese, corn, green onions, chili peppers, and sweet pepper.

In a medium mixing bowl beat together the buttermilk, egg whites, whole egg, and garlic salt with a rotary beater or wire whisk. Pour over tortilla mixture.

Bake, uncovered, in a 325° oven about 40 minutes or until a knife inserted near the center comes out clean. Let stand for 5 minutes before serving. To serve, cut into triangles. If desired, garnish with parsley. Serve with salsa. Makes 4 servings.

*Note: You may substitute ½ cup refrigerated or frozen egg product, thawed, for the egg whites and whole egg.

Total Fat:	8 g
Daily Value Fat:	12%
Saturated Fat:	4 g
Daily Value Saturated Fat:	20%

**Nutrition Facts
Per Serving:**

Calories	281
Total Fat	8 g
Saturated Fat	4 g
Cholesterol	71 mg
Sodium	653 mg
Carbohydrate	36 g
Fiber	0 g
Protein	18 g

Exchanges:
2 Starch
1 Medium-Fat Meat
1 Vegetable

Prep time: 25 minutes   Baking time: 40 minutes   Standing time: 5 minutes

Minestrone

Minestrone means "big soup" in Italian, and this bountiful bean and vegetable stew lives up to its name.

2 14½-ounce cans vegetable broth	1 15-ounce can great northern beans, rinsed and drained
1 14½-ounce can low-sodium stewed tomatoes, undrained	1 cup shredded cabbage
1 large potato, coarsely chopped	1 cup frozen whole kernel corn
1 medium onion, chopped	⅓ cup orzo (rosamarina)
1 stalk celery, thinly sliced	2 tablespoons grated Parmesan cheese
1 carrot, thinly sliced	
1½ teaspoons dried basil, crushed	

In a large saucepan combine the vegetable broth, the undrained tomatoes, the potato, onion, celery, carrot, and basil. Bring to boiling; reduce heat. Simmer, covered, for 10 minutes. Stir in the beans, cabbage, corn, and orzo.

Return to boiling; reduce heat. Simmer, covered, for 10 to 15 minutes more or until vegetables and pasta are just tender. To serve, ladle soup into bowls. Top each serving with Parmesan cheese. Makes 6 servings.

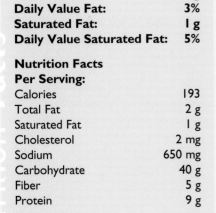

Start to finish: 55 minutes

Blue Cheese And Bean Salad

The homemade croutons make this salad special. If you like, you can substitute other cheeses for the blue cheese, such as goat cheese or freshly shredded Parmesan cheese.

2 15-ounce cans navy beans, rinsed and drained

1 small zucchini, quartered lengthwise and cut into ¼-inch slices (1 cup)

2 small tomatoes, seeded and coarsely chopped

2 green onions, thinly sliced

⅓ cup white wine vinegar

2 tablespoons olive oil

¼ teaspoon dried Italian seasoning, crushed

⅛ teaspoon pepper

2 cups French bread cut into ¾-inch cubes
    Butter-flavored nonstick spray coating

½ teaspoon onion powder

½ teaspoon garlic powder

¼ cup crumbled blue cheese (1 ounce)

In a large mixing bowl combine the navy beans, zucchini, tomatoes, and green onions.

For dressing, in a screw-top jar combine the vinegar, olive oil, Italian seasoning, and pepper. Cover and shake well. Pour dressing over bean mixture, tossing to coat. Cover and chill for 4 to 24 hours, stirring once or twice.

For croutons, before serving salad, arrange the bread cubes in a single layer in a 15×10×1-inch baking pan. Spray bread cubes with nonstick coating; toss to coat. Sprinkle with onion powder and garlic powder; toss to coat. Bake in a 350° oven for 5 to 7 minutes or until golden brown, stirring twice. Add the croutons and blue cheese to the bean mixture; toss gently. Serve immediately. Makes 6 servings.

Prep time: 15 minutes   **Chilling time:** 4 hours   **Baking time:** 5 minutes

Roasted Hot Potato Salad

This robust main dish showcases garlic-roasted vegetables tossed with a warm sweet-sour dressing. It may remind you of hot German potato salad.

Nonstick spray coating
2 pounds whole tiny new potatoes, quartered
1 cup packaged, peeled baby carrots
3 tablespoons lemon juice
1 tablespoon olive oil
1 clove garlic, minced
¼ teaspoon salt
½ cup cold water
2 teaspoons all-purpose flour

2 tablespoons vinegar
2 teaspoons sugar
½ teaspoon celery seed
½ teaspoon dry mustard
¼ teaspoon salt
⅛ teaspoon pepper
1 medium onion, chopped (½ cup)
1 clove garlic, minced
4 hard-cooked eggs
Snipped fresh chives (optional)

Spray a 13×9×2-inch baking pan with nonstick coating. Combine the potatoes and carrots in prepared pan. Spread vegetables evenly in pan. Stir together the lemon juice, olive oil, 1 clove garlic, and ¼ teaspoon salt; drizzle over vegetables. Bake, covered, in a 425° oven for 30 minutes. Remove foil; stir vegetables. Bake, uncovered, for 25 to 30 minutes more or until vegetables are tender and starting to brown on edges, stirring occasionally.

Stir together the cold water and flour. Stir in the vinegar, sugar, celery seed, mustard, ¼ teaspoon salt, and pepper; set aside. Spray a large skillet with nonstick coating. Preheat the skillet over medium-high heat. Add the onion and 1 clove garlic; cook until onion is tender. Stir in the flour mixture. Cook and stir until thickened and bubbly. Add the potato mixture, gently tossing to mix. Cook, stirring gently, for 1 to 2 minutes more or until heated through. Transfer to a serving bowl.

Press 3 of the hard-cooked eggs through a wire sieve. Add sieved eggs to potato mixture, tossing to mix. Slice the remaining hard-cooked egg; arrange slices on top of salad. If desired, garnish with chives. Makes 4 servings.

Prep time: 20 minutes   **Baking time:** 55 minutes

Light
Desserts

Tiramisu
See Recipe, Page 88

There's no need to suffer any guilt here—just revel in some of the most enticing, yet healthful, desserts around.

Fresh Pear Custard Tart

Be sure to use ripe pears for this tart. Pears that are too firm or unripe will make it difficult to eat. If you're really in a pinch, substitute sliced, well-drained canned pears.

Prepare Single-Crust Pastry. For filling, in heavy medium saucepan combine sugar and 2 tablespoons cornstarch. Stir in milk. Cook and stir over medium heat until bubbly. Cook and stir for 2 minutes more. Remove from heat. Gradually stir about 1 cup hot mixture into eggs. Return all of the egg mixture to saucepan. Stir in ginger. Cook and stir until bubbly. Reduce heat. Cook and stir for 2 minutes more. Remove from heat. Stir in vanilla. Pour into baked tart shell. Cover and chill until ready to assemble.

For glaze, combine the pear nectar and 1½ teaspoons cornstarch. Cook and stir until bubbly. Cook and stir for 2 minutes more. Cover; cool to room temperature.

To assemble, peel, core, and thinly slice pears. Arrange in a concentric pattern over filling. Pour cooled glaze over pears, spreading evenly. Cover and chill for 1 to 4 hours. To serve, top with berries. If desired, dust with sifted powdered sugar and garnish with fresh mint leaves and edible flowers. Makes 10 servings.

Single-Crust Pastry: Combine 1¼ cups all-purpose flour and ¼ teaspoon salt. Combine ¼ cup fat-free milk and 3 tablespoons cooking oil; add to flour mixture. Stir with a fork until a dough forms. Form into a ball. On a lightly floured surface, roll dough from center to edge into a 13-inch circle. Ease into an 11-inch tart pan with removable bottom. Trim to edge of pan. Prick bottom and side well with fork. Bake in a 450° oven for 10 to 12 minutes or until golden. Cool in pan on a wire rack.

Prep time: 1 hour   **Chilling time:** 1 hour

Nutrition Facts

Total Fat:	6 g
Daily Value Fat:	9%
Saturated Fat:	1 g
Daily Value Saturated Fat:	5%

Nutrition Facts
Per Serving:

Calories	216
Total Fat	6 g
Saturated Fat	1 g
Cholesterol	44 mg
Sodium	96 mg
Carbohydrate	37 g
Fiber	2 g
Protein	5 g

Exchanges:
1 Starch
1½ Fruit
1 Fat

Frozen Cranberry Pie

To soften the ice cream, place it in a chilled bowl and stir with a wooden spoon just until it is soft enough to stir in the remaining ingredients. If the ice cream becomes too soft, the pie will be icy instead of creamy.

Nonstick spray coating
6 chocolate wafer cookies, finely crushed (about ⅓ cup)
1 quart vanilla low-fat or light ice cream
1 cup whole-berry cranberry sauce
1 teaspoon finely shredded orange peel
Sugared cranberries (optional)*
Orange peel twists (optional)

Spray a 9-inch pie plate with nonstick coating. Coat the pie plate with the crushed cookies. Set aside.

In a chilled medium mixing bowl stir the ice cream with a wooden spoon just until softened. Fold in the cranberry sauce and finely shredded orange peel until combined. Spoon mixture into prepared pie plate. Cover and freeze for at least 4 hours or until firm.

To serve, cut the pie into wedges. If desired, garnish with sugared cranberries and orange peel twists. Makes 8 servings.

*Note: To make sugared cranberries, roll frozen cranberries in sugar.

Nutrition Facts

Total Fat:	3 g
Daily Value Fat:	5%
Saturated Fat:	1 g
Daily Value Saturated Fat:	5%

Nutrition Facts
Per Serving:

Calories	176
Total Fat	3 g
Saturated Fat	1 g
Cholesterol	11 mg
Sodium	83 mg
Carbohydrate	36 g
Fiber	1 g
Protein	2 g

Exchanges:
1 Starch
1 Fruit
½ Fat

Prep time: 20 minutes   **Freezing time:** 4 hours

Tiramisu

We've simplified the classic tiramisu (tee-rah-MEE-su) by using a purchased angel food cake. Most important, it's as light as a feather. Just by using lower-fat products, this slimmer version saves 14 grams fat and 200 calories per serving from the original recipe. (Also pictured on pages 84–85.)

Nutrition Facts	
Total Fat:	5 g
Daily Value Fat:	7%
Saturated Fat:	4 g
Daily Value Saturated Fat:	20%

Nutrition Facts
Per Serving:

Calories	155
Total Fat	5 g
Saturated Fat	4 g
Cholesterol	11 mg
Sodium	203 mg
Carbohydrate	21 g
Fiber	0 g
Protein	3 g

Exchanges:
1½ Starch
1 Fat

1 8-ounce package light cream cheese (Neufchâtel), softened
½ cup sifted powdered sugar
3 tablespoons coffee liqueur
1 8-ounce container light, frozen whipped dessert topping, thawed
¼ cup fat-free dairy sour cream

2 tablespoons coffee liqueur
1 8- to 10-inch round angel food cake
¼ cup strong black coffee
2 tablespoons coffee liqueur
   Mocha Fudge Sauce (optional)
   Edible flowers (optional)

For filling, in a large bowl combine the cream cheese, powdered sugar, and the 3 tablespoons liqueur; beat with an electric mixer on medium speed until blended and smooth. Stir in ½ cup of the whipped dessert topping. Set aside.

For the frosting, in another bowl combine the remaining whipped dessert topping, the sour cream, and 2 tablespoons liqueur. Set aside.

Using a serrated knife, cut the angel food cake horizontally into 3 layers. Place 1 layer on a serving platter and 2 layers on large dinner plates. With a long-tined fork or a skewer, poke holes in tops of all 3 layers. In a small bowl combine the coffee and 2 tablespoons liqueur; drizzle over all layers. Spread the first layer with half of the filling. Add a second layer and spread with the remaining filling. Add top layer of cake. Frost cake with the frosting. (If desired, cover and chill for up to 4 hours.)

If desired, just before serving, drizzle top and sides with Mocha Fudge Sauce. To serve, drizzle dessert plates with more sauce (if desired), cut cake into wedges, and top each plate with a cake slice. If desired, garnish with edible flowers. Makes 16 servings.

Mocha Fudge Sauce: In a small bowl dissolve 1 teaspoon instant coffee crystals in 1 teaspoon hot water; stir in ¼ cup chocolate-flavored syrup.

Start to finish: 25 minutes

Gingered Peach And Pear Crisp

You get a double dose of ginger with each bite of this luscious dessert. Grated fresh ginger flavors the fruit filling, and gingersnaps, combined with rolled oats, form the crumb topping.

1 16-ounce can peach slices (juice pack), drained	1 teaspoon grated fresh ginger
1 16-ounce can pear halves (juice pack), drained and cut up	½ cup finely crushed gingersnaps
	½ cup quick-cooking rolled oats
	2 tablespoons brown sugar

In an 8-inch quiche dish or 8×1½-inch round baking pan place the peaches, pears, and ginger. Toss to combine.

In a small mixing bowl stir together the gingersnaps, oats, and brown sugar. Sprinkle evenly over fruit. Bake in a 425° oven for 15 to 20 minutes or until heated through. Makes 6 servings.

Prep time: 12 minutes   **Baking time:** 15 minutes

Brownie-Fruit Pizza

To make the brownie crust easier to cut, spray a pizza cutter or knife with nonstick spray coating.

Nonstick spray coating
½ cup sugar
3 tablespoons margarine or butter, softened
¼ cup refrigerated or frozen egg product, thawed
¾ cup chocolate-flavored syrup
⅔ cup all-purpose flour

3 cups fresh fruit (such as peeled, sliced, and quartered kiwifruit; sliced, peeled peaches; sliced nectarines or strawberries; red raspberries; and/or blueberries)
½ cup chocolate-flavored syrup

Spray a 12-inch pizza pan with nonstick coating. Set aside.

For crust, in a medium mixing bowl combine sugar and margarine or butter. Beat with an electric mixer on medium speed until creamy. Add egg product; beat well. Alternately add the ¾ cup chocolate-flavored syrup and the flour, beating after each addition on low speed until combined. Spread into the prepared pizza pan.

Bake in a 350° oven about 20 minutes or until top springs back when lightly touched. Cool in pan on a wire rack.

To serve, cut brownie into 12 wedges. Top each wedge with fruit. Drizzle with the ½ cup chocolate-flavored syrup. Makes 12 servings.

Nutrition Facts

Total Fat:	4 g
Daily Value Fat:	6%
Saturated Fat:	1 g
Daily Value Saturated Fat:	5%

Nutrition Facts
Per Serving:

Calories	169
Total Fat	4 g
Saturated Fat	1 g
Cholesterol	0 mg
Sodium	60 mg
Carbohydrate	35 g
Fiber	1 g
Protein	2 g

Exchanges:
1 Starch
1 Fruit
1 Fat

Prep time: 15 minutes   **Baking time:** 20 minutes

Biscotti

A specialty of coffeehouses, these twice-baked Italian cookies make a great snack. With fewer than 40 calories and only 1 gram of fat each, they can curb your sweet tooth without causing you pangs of guilt.

Nonstick spray coating
2 cups all-purpose flour
2 teaspoons baking powder
2 teaspoons anise seed, crushed
1 teaspoon finely shredded
   lemon peel

¼ cup margarine or butter
½ cup sugar
2 eggs

Spray a large cookie sheet with nonstick coating. Set aside. In a medium mixing bowl stir together the flour, baking powder, anise seed, and lemon peel. Set aside.

In a small mixing bowl beat margarine or butter with an electric mixer on medium speed for 30 seconds. Add sugar; beat until combined. Add eggs; beat well. Stir in flour mixture.

On waxed paper shape dough into two 12-inch-long logs. Place logs on prepared cookie sheet; flatten logs slightly.

Bake in a 375° oven for 15 to 20 minutes or until lightly browned. Cool completely on wire racks (about 1 hour).

Cut each log into ½-inch-thick slices. Arrange the slices, cut sides down, on the cookie sheet. Bake in a 325° oven for 8 minutes. Turn over. Bake for 8 to 10 minutes more or until crisp and light brown. Transfer to wire racks and cool completely. Makes 48 cookies.

Prep time: 25 minutes **Baking time:** 31 minutes **Cooling time:** 2 hours

Watermelon Sherbet

This refreshing after-dinner treat is a welcome change from fat-laden ice creams.

4 cups cubed, seeded watermelon	I envelope unflavored gelatin
½ cup sugar	⅓ cup cranberry juice

Place watermelon cubes in a blender container or food processor bowl. Cover and blend or process until smooth. (There should be 3 cups of the watermelon mixture.) Stir in sugar.

In a small saucepan combine the gelatin and cranberry juice. Let mixture stand for 5 minutes. Stir mixture over low heat until gelatin is dissolved.

Stir the gelatin mixture into the melon mixture. Pour into an 8×8×2-inch baking pan. Cover and freeze about 2 hours or until firm.

Break up frozen mixture and place in a chilled mixer bowl. Beat with an electric mixer on medium to high speed until mixture is fluffy. Return to pan. Cover and freeze about 6 hours or until firm. Makes 8 (½-cup) servings.

Prep time: 25 minutes   **Freezing time:** 8 hours

Tropical Fruit Compote

Make a simple fruit compote extra special by garnishing with an edible flower, such as geranium, violet, pansy, or nasturtium. Use only those flowers that have not been treated with pesticides.

⅓ cup unsweetened pineapple juice

3 tablespoons sugar

1 teaspoon finely shredded lime or lemon peel (set aside)

3 tablespoons lime or lemon juice

3 whole cloves

3 inches stick cinnamon, broken

3 cardamom pods, opened (optional)

1 papaya or mango, peeled, seeded, and thinly sliced

1 kiwifruit, peeled and sliced

1 carambola (star fruit), sliced

1 cup fresh pineapple chunks

1 banana, sliced

Lime peel strips (optional)

Edible flowers (optional)

In a small saucepan stir together the pineapple juice, sugar, and lime or lemon juice. Add the cloves, cinnamon, and cardamom pods (if desired).

Bring to boiling, stirring until sugar dissolves; reduce heat. Simmer, covered, for 10 minutes. Remove from heat. Let stand about 10 minutes to cool slightly. Sieve to remove spices; discard spices. Stir shredded lime or lemon peel into liquid.

Meanwhile, in a large mixing bowl toss together the papaya or mango, kiwifruit, carambola, pineapple, and banana. Pour juice mixture over fruit; stir gently to coat. Cover and let stand about 30 minutes, stirring once or twice.

To serve, spoon fruit and juices into small dessert dishes. If desired, garnish with lime peel strips and edible flowers. Makes 4 servings.

Prep time: 30 minutes **Standing time:** 30 minutes

Berries with Zabaglione

Similar to a custard sauce, zabaglione can be served with many desserts. This version contains a little sour cream for a slight tang.

2 tablespoons sugar
2 teaspoons cornstarch
¾ cup fat-free milk
1 beaten egg
¼ cup light dairy sour cream
2 tablespoons sweet or dry Marsala

2 cups fresh berries (such as red raspberries, blackberries, blueberries, and/or halved strawberries)
Ground cinnamon or ground nutmeg (optional)
Fresh mint (optional)

For custard, in a heavy medium saucepan combine sugar and cornstarch. Stir in milk. Cook and stir over medium heat until mixture is thickened and bubbly. Cook and stir for 2 minutes more. Remove from heat. Gradually stir about half of the hot mixture into the beaten egg. Return all of the egg mixture to the saucepan. Cook until nearly bubbly, but do not boil. Immediately pour custard into a bowl; stir in sour cream and Marsala. Cover the surface with plastic wrap. Chill for 2 to 24 hours.

To serve, divide the berries evenly among 4 dessert dishes. Spoon custard evenly over the berries. If desired, sprinkle with cinnamon or nutmeg and garnish with mint. Serve immediately. Makes 4 servings.

Total Fat:	5 g
Daily Value Fat:	7%
Saturated Fat:	2 g
Daily Value Saturated Fat:	10%

Nutrition Facts
Per Serving:

Calories	136
Total Fat	5 g
Saturated Fat	2 g
Cholesterol	61 mg
Sodium	48 mg
Carbohydrate	19 g
Fiber	2 g
Protein	4 g

Exchanges:
1½ Fruit
1 Fat

Prep time: 15 minutes **Chilling time:** 2 hours

Index